ACTIVITIES FOR RESPONSIVE CAREGIVING

Also by Jean Barbre, EdD

**BABY STEPS TO STEM: INFANT AND TODDLER
SCIENCE, TECHNOLOGY, ENGINEERING, AND
MATH ACTIVITIES**

**FOUNDATIONS OF RESPONSIVE CAREGIVING:
INFANTS, TODDLERS, AND TWOS**

Activities
for
Responsive
Caregiving

Infants,
Toddlers,
and Twos

JEAN BARBRE, EdD

Redleaf Press®
www.redleafpress.org
800-423-8309

Published by Redleaf Press
10 Yorkton Court
St. Paul, MN 55117
www.redleafpress.org

First edition 2013
Cover design by Jim Handrigan
Cover photographs © Ocean Photography/Veer
Interior design by Percolator
Typeset in ITC Stone Serif
Printed in the United States of America

Interior photographs by Shawn Thomas, except on page 15 © iStockphoto.com/Kevin Klöpper;
page 25 © iStockphoto.com/Darrell Fraser; page 86 © iStockphoto.com/Christopher Futcher;
and page 119 © iStockphoto.com/alarich

Library of Congress Cataloging-in-Publication Data
Barbre, Jean.
    Activities for responsive caregiving : infants, toddlers, and twos / Jean Barbre.
      p. cm.
    Summary: "Activities for Responsive Caregiving is filled with more than 80 developmentally
appropriate activities and experiences that help young children acquire skills, build positive
relationships, and optimize their intellectual, social, emotional, and physical development.
This resource also provides strategies that support your role as a responsive caregiver" —
Provided by publisher.
    ISBN 978-1-60554-084-9 (pbk.)
    1. Child care. 2. Early childhood education. 3. Child development. 4. Parent and infant.
5. Parent and child.   I. Title.
HQ778.5.B36 2012
649'.1—dc23
                         2012025633

Printed on acid-free paper   U18-08

To Kim and Kat:

*My most cherished role in life
is being your mother. You are
my joy and inspiration.*

Contents

Acknowledgments

I have many people to thank for helping make this book possible. First, I want to thank my family for their support and encouragement. To my husband, thank you for supporting my efforts to give back to the field of early education. Your help in cooking meals, helping around the house, and printing photos allowed me the time I needed to create and write the activities in this book. To my daughters, Kim and Kat, thank you for your interest in and excitement about my writing. To my mother, brother, and sister, thank you for always being my greatest champions. Thanks to my friend Ingrid Anderson for your support on this book. A special thanks to Kimberly Bohannon for your creativity and willingness to contribute your songs and chants. Your sense of humor and playfulness has added to the joy of writing this book. To Shawn Thomas, thank you for your photography and creativity. It has been a pleasure to capture the images of children from birth to age three with you.

To the staff of the Orange Coast College Harry and Grace Steele Children's Center and the Hatsue Daman Family Child Care Center, thank you for allowing me to photograph your amazing early child care programs. To my friend Stacy Deeble-Reynolds, thank you for letting me take photographs in your home. And a special thanks to my friends and colleagues who let me photograph their beautiful children.

I thank the editorial team at Redleaf Press, especially the work of Jeanne Engelmann and Kyra Ostendorf. Your ideas and direction provided focus to the book. To the creative team at Redleaf Press, thank you for making the activities come to life through formatting and images. And to you, the reader of this book: You are important in the lives of very young children. You make a tremendous difference in their growth and development. As a responsive caregiver, you help children begin their lives in loving, caring, and nurturing environments. My goal in creating the activities in this book is to make them easy and fun to incorporate into your program. Infant and toddlerhood are amazing times of discovery and exploration. I hope you will enjoy expanding children's learning through the playful activities in this book.

Introduction

Very young children are rapidly changing and discovering their worlds; their first three years set the stage for a lifetime of learning. As a responsive caregiver, you devise activities and experiences to help them develop. You help them acquire skills and master developmental milestones. And by engaging them, you foster the relationships that help them develop trust. In other words, how you care for young children dramatically affects their lifelong intellectual, emotional, social, and physical development.

RESPONSIVE CAREGIVERS

What exactly *is* a responsive caregiver? The term *caregiver* describes any adult who provides care for children. You might be a parent, grandparent, aunt, uncle, neighbor, family child care provider, or program staff member—whatever your relationship to a child, if it's ongoing, you're a caregiver. *Responsive caregivers* go further: You make a point of addressing each child's individual needs in developmentally appropriate ways. You provide not only *care* tailored to each child—you also provide it in a loving, nurturing, stable *setting*.

One of your chief responsibilities as a responsive caregiver is planning activities to help children become skilled across four learning domains: social-emotional, physical, cognitive, and language. Another is using unplanned opportunities—what are often called *teachable moments*—to help children learn new things and build on their existing knowledge. As a responsive caregiver, you also design settings for learning, where children can explore, discover, and create their own ways of learning. You're sensitive to how they learn, and you offer them lots of ways to do so at every stage of their growth and development.

COMPONENTS OF HIGH-QUALITY EARLY CARE AND EDUCATION

High-quality early care programs provide children with activities that reinforce what they already know and then build on that knowledge. No single indicator for quality exists, but excellent programs consistently adhere to several principles:

- Children and caregivers enjoy ongoing, nurturing relationships.

- Children are assigned to individual primary caregivers.

- Children's individual needs are respected.

- Children learn in play-based settings.

- Activities are age and stage appropriate.

- Environments are physically safe.

- Children's new challenges build on their existing knowledge or skills.

- Children are offered experiences that build skills across all developmental domains.

- Schedules and routines are tailored to individual children.

- Staff talk and cooperate with parents in culturally sensitive ways.

If you work in a high-quality early care and education program, you already have the knowledge and expertise to provide the care I've just described. You know how to give infants, toddlers, and two-year-olds, including children with special needs, the experiences they need to grow. If you are new to high-quality care, my companion book, *Foundations of Responsive Caregiving: Infants, Toddlers, and Twos,* offers you the key principles of infant and toddler growth and development. Reading it can acquaint you with recent research on early learning and your role in helping children develop. *Foundations of Responsive Caregiving* explores strategies you can use to help very young children learn: attachment theories, brain development, designing the environment, developmentally appropriate practices, curriculum planning, observations, and assessments. *Foundations of Responsive Caregiving* can also help you create learning environments in which children can joyfully explore the world.

This book has a different goal: it takes what I present in *Foundations of Responsive Caregiving* and applies it to day-to-day play activities. This book shows you how to use the principles and theories in *Foundations of Responsive Caregiving* as underpinnings for activities that promote learning across the four learning domains. Each of the activities is easy and fun; each engages children playfully in learning new skills.

It's my hope that you'll enjoy some discoveries of your own while you're helping children test their newfound abilities and curiosity. As a responsive caregiver, you can make a big difference in the lives of young children.

Setting the Stage for Activities

As an early childhood professional, you know that high-quality settings are essential to children's growth and development. To create such environments, your program must factor in safety, materials, design, and the importance of adapting activities to the needs of every child. Most important, it must emphasize the centrality of *play*. This book offers activities you can select or adapt to encourage learning through play.

Play is the business of childhood. It's through play that children engage their minds and bodies. Play teaches them new skills, including role playing and conceptualizing. Young children are naturally curious, and they enjoy experimenting with the world around them. You can promote early learning by engaging them in activities that increase their skills and competencies. Selecting suitable materials, including toys and books, is an important first step in creating activities for a high-quality, play-based program.

SAFETY

You should always consider safety when you're selecting toys and planning activities for young children. Be sure that any manufactured items used by infants, toddlers, and twos are labeled by their producers as age-appropriate. All toys should be durable, easy to clean, and large enough that they—or pieces of them—cannot be swallowed or cause choking. As you know, children under age three explore the world through their senses, and they put everything in their mouths. This puts them at high risk for swallowing and choking on things. You can buy baby-care devices that assess the size of objects to determine if they're too small for infants or toddlers to play with or might pose choking hazards. Don't allow infants and toddlers to play with small objects like marbles, small balls, or toys that break down easily into smaller pieces. Don't acquire toys with sharp edges, points, encased liquids, or materials that could break apart when mouthed or bitten.

Make sure that manufactured products have been carefully tested and are nontoxic. Toy animals and dolls should not have glued-on or stapled parts (for example, wigs or eyes). Always remove paper tags before offering the toys to children. The Art and Creative Materials Institute (ACMI) is a terrific safety resource: it lists art, craft, and creative materials that are safe and nontoxic for children to use. Use only those art and craft materials bearing ACMI's Approved Product (AP) seal of approval. Learn more about ACMI and safe materials at www.acmiart.org.

When you're acquiring plastic toys or baby bottles, you have your homework ahead of you! You need to make sure they're made from thick, durable, heavy plastic that's free from the toxic chemical bisphenol A (BPA). They should be labeled *BPA-free*. It's also important to minimize the risk to children from lead-contaminated or toxic products by buying (or accepting as donations) only those items that meet the United States Consumer Product Safety Commission's standards. Regularly consult the commission's list of toys that have been recalled, available at www.cpsc.gov /Recalls. The manufacturers' association Toy Safety Association, Inc., also addresses toy safety at www.toyassociation.org.

Infants and toddlers need to be well supervised at all times, and that also goes for the objects they play with. Check toys frequently. Items that are broken or chipped can pose dangers to young children and should be repaired or thrown out. Toys should be cleaned or sanitized frequently, according to your program's policies. Eliminate any toys or objects with strings or cords attached. Water tables and other containers used for water play should be closely supervised; sadly, children can drown in just a few inches of water.

SELECTING MATERIALS

The classroom toys and objects you select should meet the developmental needs of children from birth to age three. In other words, they should provide learning opportunities across the four developmental domains: social-emotional, physical, cognitive, and language. (You'll learn more about age-appropriate materials when I discuss specific activities and the learning domains they support.)

As a responsive caregiver, you want to promote cooperation and sharing among children, so do two things as soon as possible. First, take an inventory of play materi-

als and toys that aren't being used much by the children, remove them for a while, and then reintroduce them to the children. Most children find new uses for familiar objects once their skills, knowledge, and imaginations have increased. Give those neglected toys another chance! Second, be sure that you have enough of especially popular items to prevent fights over them. Most young children play with a variety of toys during the day, but on those occasions when a number of children want to play with the same thing, you should have enough of those toys on hand to prevent behavioral problems.

DESIGNING THE ENVIRONMENT

You already recognize the importance of creating high-quality learning environments. In my companion book, *Foundations of Responsive Caregiving: Infants, Toddlers, and Twos,* I present the principles of designing such environments. Many other books can help you design and improve your indoor and outdoor environments. I encourage you to delve more deeply into this topic; I can't overstress its importance.

Here, I'll simply say this: high-quality early care programs apply universal design to their settings. Universal design for learning (UDL) is a concept developed by the Center for Applied Special Technology. Its importance to early education programs lies in its foundational premises: children learn in different ways, and learning environments must be designed to accommodate all children, including those with special needs and/or disabilities.

What does this mean, exactly? Using UDL means that your indoor and outdoor settings allow children to learn from more than one source. Children learn through their senses and by having multiple experiences in their environment. For example, children have different learning experiences when they play in the block and dramatic play areas. An environment created with UDL can be adapted to meet the needs of all children. Tables and chairs are the correct size and height for the age group and can be easily accessed by all children. The floor surfaces are comfortable for infants and toddlers to roll on, crawl on, and move across with ease. Well-designed small-group spaces and center areas are inviting; they encourage adults and children to work together on projects, build friendships, talk to each other, and play without unwelcome interruptions.

LEARNING DOMAINS

Children develop and learn best in settings that are developmentally and age appropriate. As a responsive caregiver, you help children move toward skills in the four chief learning domains primarily through play. I discuss each learning domain briefly here; much more about them can be found in *Foundations of Responsive Caregiving: Infants, Toddlers, and Twos*. Collectively, the play activities in this book support all of these areas of development; I've noted which ones are primary at the beginning of each activity.

Social-Emotional Development

Understanding oneself and others is what we call *social-emotional development*. Such understanding is essential to young children's well-being. They learn social and emotional skills simultaneously, and they learn them through their relationships with adults and peers. As a responsive caregiver, you help children develop a healthy sense of self, personal identity, positive relationships with adults and other children, self-regulation, empathy, caring for others, and sharing. That's a lot!

Physical Development

During their first three years, children's physical and sensory skills develop rapidly. They learn, move, and explore the world through their senses, using their gross- and fine-motor skills. As a responsive caregiver, you're attuned to their physical needs—everything from feeding babies to providing plenty of open space in which two-year-olds can run and climb. You take into account the changes in children's physical abilities, and you applaud them when they become more mobile, first sitting up, then crawling, then walking, eating, and dressing all by themselves.

But of course this isn't all there is to their early development: while they're mastering new physical skills, they're also increasing their ability to perceive and conceptualize. *Perceptual development* is what we call the ability to organize our senses and our sensory experiences. As children's perception grows, they understand the world better. Interestingly, there's a link between perceptual and motor skills that's unique among the ways the domains are connected to each other. Gross-motor skills, which involve the large muscles of the body, develop through big movements like jumping, dancing, and marching. Fine-motor skills are honed by learning to control the muscles and movements of hands and fingers. As children develop these skills, their ability to perceive the world increases; their competencies become more refined and sophisticated.

Cognitive Development

We call the thinking and learning that begins at birth and continues throughout life *cognitive development.* As children's ability to think, reason, and problem solve increases, they better understand how the world works. They broaden their thinking and test out new ideas. You can see this in the way they make use of their growing cognitive skills: they can soon wield cause and effect, memory, spatial awareness, connecting experiences, awareness of numbers, imitating others, progression of play, and following simple directions.

Language Development

Integrating sounds and language is termed *language development.* Learning language is *the* universal task of children from birth to age three. From earliest infancy, children play with sounds and language. As a responsive caregiver, you look for chances to encourage language development by listening, speaking, and reading to children. You know that acquiring language is significantly linked to literacy, and you help children build this skill by learning sounds, symbols, and patterns of speech.

You can help infants, toddlers, and twos build vocabulary by asking open-ended questions and modeling appropriate use of language. Children develop expressive and receptive language skills by hearing their caregivers talk, read, and sing to them throughout the day. Encourage language development by playing with rhythm, rhyme, and music; with chants and fingerplays; and with printed materials. Immersing young children in these language-rich activities helps them learn how to communicate their needs, connect language with real-world knowledge, and understand

and use conceptual language. I can't overstress the importance of books as tools for introducing new concepts and language.

HOW TO USE THIS BOOK

I created the 101 activities in this book to promote young children's learning across the four developmental domains. You can use any of these activities indoors or outdoors. If I think an activity is better suited to one area of your classroom or to a time of day, such as small-group or circle time, I have noted this. Each activity includes detailed information about its developmental potential:

- Recommended Age

- Learning Outcomes
  - Social-Emotional Development
  - Physical Development
  - Cognitive Development
  - Language Development

- Materials
  - Suggested Books

- How to Do It
  - Modifications for Twos
  - Expand the Activity

- Building Language Skills
  - Vocabulary
  - Questions and Things to Say
  - Songs, Chants, and Fingerplays

The primary learning outcomes for each activity are indicated with a ✱. These symbols represent the activity's target for learning and development. Secondary learning outcomes are listed as well. Activities to help children learn across developmental domains can be selected on the basis of primary or secondary learning outcomes. For example, suppose you want to focus on social-emotional development: appendix A lists activities by learning domain. Use it to select activities that support specific learning, foster developmental competencies, and integrate children's learning.

Some activities work better for infants than for older children and vice versa, so each activity specifies a recommended age: infant, toddler, or infant and toddler. You will see an icon on the top right-hand corner of each activity indicating the recommended age group for each activity. Activities for toddlers can be great for two-year-olds. Every activity includes modifications for making them more stimulating for two-year-olds. The children in your care have a range of abilities, so you may need to modify some of the activities to accommodate several developmental stages.

All of the activities include a list of suggested books and either a song or a chant. As mentioned earlier, reading is important, and so is singing.

Books and Print

Young children build their vocabularies and learn the rules of language through constant exposure to words and print. High-quality early education programs make language development and reading key components—and books lie at their center. Books not only draw children into language and literacy, they also help them learn about the world. Best practices include placing books in every area where children spend time, including outdoor spaces. Best practices also tell us that books with realistic pictures (rather than cartoons or drawings) work best.

Select books that are age appropriate and that meet the developmental needs of the children you care for. Babies savor books by placing them in their mouths, so infants' books should be sturdy, texturally stimulating (cloth and/or chunky), and easily cleaned. The youngest children enjoy word-free books; these stimulate their imaginations and prompt imaginative storytelling and creative interpreting by adults and children alike. Once children understand a bit about the relationship between words and print and have built up their language and cognitive skills, they enjoy books with simple text and large print, such as *The Very Hungry Caterpillar* by Eric Carle. As a caregiver, you should point to the words and read slowly to emphasize the relationship between spoken words and print on the page.

Printed materials found at home and in the community also help children learn about language. Call children's attention to the signs outside their classrooms, the words and symbols on street signs, and classroom area labels, such as "Library and Art Area." By the time they're toddlers or twos, children begin to recognize the colors and shapes of words they see regularly; they're learning that print is all around them.

You can't reread a favorite book too often! Children respond well to picture books and stories with rhymes and repetition—for example, *Brown Bear, Brown Bear, What Do You See?* and *Chicka Chicka Boom Boom*, both by Bill Martin Jr. Silly words and pictures make reading and language development fun. Be sure that your reading to young children is two-way: ask them simple open-ended questions about the pictures and what you've read; encourage them to identify colors and what's in the illustrations. Such active reading teaches children new vocabulary, helps correct developing language errors, and expands learning opportunities. We call this approach to reading *dialogic reading*.

Dialogic reading engages children actively in what might otherwise be a passive activity: being read to. Instead, children ask and answer questions about what they hear and see; they turn the pages of the book. They learn language by storytelling and talking with you, their caregiver. They become invested in reading when they become invested in their relationship with you. Their interest in print grows whenever they learn or repeat new words and identify objects. Best practices include reading to the children in your care for at least fifteen to twenty minutes every day. In addition, you should make sure that books appear everywhere in your program.

Songs, Chants, and Fingerplays

Songs, chants, and fingerplays promote language development too. Babies and toddlers love listening to adults sing to and teach them songs and nursery rhymes.

Rhythm-driven songs and rhymes bring joy to young children—they learn to associate that joy with language. While the youngest children in your care may not understand the meaning of your songs and rhymes, they can nonetheless delight in singing and playing with words. You can teach rhythm by encouraging children to clap along with a song or to shake or tap a musical instrument. Fingerplays like "Itsy, Bitsy Spider" and "Pat-a-Cake" offer them the chance to develop fine-motor skills while learning language. Playful songs, chants, and fingerplays teach infants, toddlers, and twos to discern units of speech and to blend sounds through music. Constant immersion in language strengthens their ability to learn language's many meanings and sets the stage for literacy.

All the activities in this book are accompanied by suggestions for vocabulary, books to use, and questions to ask. Appendix B lists books I recommend by the learning domains they best address. I hope you'll enjoy adapting my suggestions to the children in your care. Your creativity and imagination will expand their lives!

FINAL THOUGHTS

As a responsive caregiver, you play a critical role in the growth and development of infants, toddlers, and two-year-olds. Children are naturally curious, and they love to experiment with and explore the environment. You build on their curiosity by planning and providing play-based activities. And you understand that healthy relationships lie at the heart of children's developing skills and competencies.

I created the activities in this book to strengthen your understanding of how children grow and learn. Every one of these 101 activities stresses the importance of responsive caregiving. Every one of them demonstrates how learning can be integrated across learning domains. I hope the play activities I've devised motivate and inspire you in your efforts to provide high-quality, loving care for young children. I encourage you to use your own creativity to build and expand on my work, to tailor it to every child you care for. Each child is unique, as you know, and each one learns best in a loving, caring, valuing environment.

Nothing is quite as sweet or precious as young children are. The first three years of children's lives are so exciting. I hope the beautiful young children in your care prompt you to try the activities in this book. And I hope this book supports you and your program in offering quality activities to infants, toddlers, and two-year-olds.

All About Baby

MATERIALS

Suggested Books

- *Baby da Vinci: My Body* by Julie Aigner-Clark
- *Eyes and Nose, Fingers and Toes* by Bendon Publishing
- *Head, Shoulders, Knees, and Toes* by Annie Kubler
- *My First Body Board Book* by DK Publishing
- *The Pudgy Where Is Your Nose? Book* by Laura Rader
- *Where Is Baby's Belly Button?* by Karen Katz

HOW TO DO IT

Lay the baby on her back on a blanket or sit with her in your lap. Start by touching or holding her feet and naming them. While you name the feet, rub or lightly tickle them. Then touch or hold her legs and name them. Progress up her body, naming the body parts you touch or hold, such as her knees, tummy, fingers, hands, arms, mouth, nose, and eyes. End by gently touching or stroking her head and naming it. Read the suggested books, introduce the vocabulary words, and sing and chant with the infant.

Modifications for Toddlers and Twos

Sit on the floor with the children facing you. Touch your own body parts as you name them and invite the children to do the same. For example, say, "Here are my hands. Where are your hands? Let's clap our hands together."

Expand the Activity

While children play throughout the day or as you perform everyday routines—such as dressing and undressing the baby—name the body parts you touch or hold. For example, name her hands and arms as you slip them inside her sweater, and name her toes and feet as you place them in her socks or shoes.

LEARNING OUTCOMES

SOCIAL-EMOTIONAL DEVELOPMENT
- ✶ Sense of self
- Personal identity

PHYSICAL DEVELOPMENT
- Perception

COGNITIVE DEVELOPMENT
- Memory
- Connecting experiences
- Imitating others

LANGUAGE DEVELOPMENT
- ✶ Concept words
- Receptive language
- Connecting words with real-world knowledge
- Using language in play

BUILD LANGUAGE SKILLS

Vocabulary

- Feet
- Legs
- Knees
- Tummy
- Belly button
- Fingers
- Hands
- Arms
- Chin
- Mouth
- Nose
- Eyes
- Ears
- Head
- Hair

Questions and Things to Say

"Where are your toes? Oh! Here are your toes!" (Touch each toe one by one.) "Where are your hands? Oh! Here are your hands!" (Clap the baby's hands together while saying "hands.") "Where is your nose? Can you wiggle your nose like this?" (Wiggle your nose.)

Songs, Chants, and Fingerplays

Song: "Where Are Baby's Feet?"
by Kimberly Bohannon
(Tune: "Frère Jacques")

Where are baby's feet?
Where are baby's feet?
Here they are.
Here they are.

Wiggle your toes.
Wiggle your toes.
Tickle your feet.
Tickle your feet.

Where are baby's hands?
Where are baby's hands?
Here they are.
Here they are.

Wiggle your fingers.
Wiggle your fingers.
Clap your hands.
Clap your hands.

Song: "Smiling Baby" by Jean Barbre
(Tune: "Frère Jacques")

Smiling baby,
Smiling baby,
Here you are.
Here you are.
You're a special baby.
You're a special baby.
Yes, you are.
Yes, you are.

Song: "Head, Shoulders, Knees, and Toes"
(traditional)

Song: "Hokey Pokey" (traditional)

Another Reason to Smile

MATERIALS

– Small hand mirror

Suggested Books

– *Baby Faces* by Margaret Miller
– *Eyes, Nose, Fingers, and Toes: A First Book All About You* by Judy Hindley
– *Hello! Good-bye!* by Aliki
– *A Splendid Friend, Indeed* by Suzanne Bloom
– *Two Eyes, a Nose, and a Mouth* by Roberta Grobel Intrater

HOW TO DO IT

One of the first social cues a baby produces is a smile. Babies will wiggle their arms and legs and smile to gain the attention of their caregivers. Encourage them to smile, and smile back at them as often as you can. When you respond to a baby's smile, enthusiastically identify your emotion, such as joy and happiness. Gently tickle the baby under her chin and see if you can get her to smile and laugh. Talking and smiling with a baby reinforces your relationship and social engagement. Talk about the baby's reflection in the mirror. Let the baby see herself in the mirror. Read the suggested books, introduce the vocabulary words, and sing and chant with the infant.

Modifications for Toddlers and Twos

Sit with a toddler in front of a large mirror. Talk to the child about her features. Point out her face, fingers, toes. Show the toddler how to wave hello, good-bye, and blow kisses.

Expand the Activity

Take photos of the children playing and smiling. Read the suggested books to them. Tell them about making friends and showing people we care about them.

LEARNING OUTCOMES

SOCIAL-EMOTIONAL DEVELOPMENT
✱ Relationships with adults
– Sense of self
– Personal identity
– Caring for others

PHYSICAL DEVELOPMENT
– Perception

COGNITIVE DEVELOPMENT
– Cause and effect
– Memory
– Imitating others
– Progression of play

LANGUAGE DEVELOPMENT
✱ Communicating needs
– Receptive language
– Expressive language

BUILD LANGUAGE SKILLS

Vocabulary

- Smile
- Smiling
- Baby
- Laughing
- Happy
- Beautiful
- Special
- Face
- Mirror

Questions and Things to Say

"Look at you smiling! You are such a special baby. I'm going to smile at you, and now you're smiling back at me. Can you smile with me? There's your beautiful smile!"

Songs, Chants, and Fingerplays

Song: "Smiling Baby" by Jean Barbre
(Tune: "Frère Jacques")

Smiling baby,
Smiling baby,
Here you are.
Here you are.
You're a special baby.
You're a special baby.
Yes, you are.
Yes, you are.

Song: "There's a Smile on Your Face" by Kimberly Bohannon
(Tune: "If You're Happy and You Know It")

There's a smile on your face,
On your face.
There's a smile on your face,
On your face.
There's a smile on your face.
And it brightens up my day.
There's a smile on your face,
On your face.

3

Babies Are Sleeping—Shhh!

MATERIALS

Suggested Books

- *All Asleep* by Joanna Walsh
- *I Love to Sleep* by Amelie Graux
- *Let's Go to Sleep!* by Patricia Geis
- *Sleep* by Roger Priddy
- *Sleep Tight!* by Sue Baker

HOW TO DO IT

Most babies develop an interest in other babies sometime during the first six months of life. While other babies are sleeping, carry an infant to their cribs or sleeping areas so she can observe them. Hold her close enough to see what the babies are doing. Talk with her quietly about the sleeping babies—for example, say that they are sleeping because they are tired from playing and that you must use a quiet voice so you don't wake them. Read the suggested books, introduce the vocabulary words, and sing and chant with the infant.

Modifications for Toddlers and Twos

Read a book about babies sleeping, such as *Sleep* by Roberta Grobel Intrater. Then take the toddler or two-year-old to observe a few babies sleeping. Talk with her in a hushed voice about the sleeping babies. Ask her questions about what the babies are doing and why they might be sleeping.

Expand the Activity

If one of the sleeping babies begins to wake up, talk about what the baby is doing that lets you know she is waking up. For example, say, "I hear something. Do you hear something? I think it might be Sasha waking up from her nap. Let's see if Sasha is waking up."

LEARNING OUTCOMES

SOCIAL-EMOTIONAL DEVELOPMENT
- ✱ Self-regulation
- ✱ Caring for others
- – Relationships with peers

PHYSICAL DEVELOPMENT
- – Perception

COGNITIVE DEVELOPMENT
- – Cause and effect
- – Memory
- – Connecting experiences
- – Imitating others
- – Following simple directions

LANGUAGE DEVELOPMENT
- – Receptive language
- – Expressive language
- – Connecting words with real-world knowledge
- – Concept words

BUILD LANGUAGE SKILLS

Vocabulary

- Sleeping
- Sleepy
- Waking up

- Blanket
- Pillow
- Crib

- Sheet
- Bottle
- Nap

- Eyes closed
- Pajamas
- Tired

- Quiet
- Noisy

Questions and Things to Say

"Shhh. Everyone is sleeping—Maya, Jack, and Tomás. They are sleeping because they are tired. Their eyes are closed. They have their blankets to keep them warm. We must be quiet so we don't wake them."

Songs, Chants, and Fingerplays

Song: "The Babies Are Sleeping"
by Kimberly Bohannon
(Tune: "It's Raining, It's Pouring")

It's naptime.
It's naptime.
The babies are sleeping.
They've closed their eyes.
They need to rest.
Shh—let's not wake them.

Song: "Baby Was Sleeping"
by Jean Barbre
(Tune: "Frère Jacques")

Baby was sleeping.
Baby was sleeping.
Watch her wake.
Watch her wake.
See the baby smiling.
See the baby smiling.
How are you?
How are you?

Baby Animal Sounds

MATERIALS

– Books with pictures of baby animals (wordless books are fine), such as those by Priddy Bicknell (for example, *Bunny and Friends* and *Duckling and Friends*)

Suggested Books

– *Animal Babies* by Stephen Cartwright
– *Baby Animals* by Garth Williams
– *Baby Animals in the Wild* by Kingfisher
– *Baby Touch and Feel Animals* by DK Publishing
– *Spot's Favorite Baby Animals* by Eric Hill
– *Touch and Feel Baby Animals* by Julie Aigner-Clark

HOW TO DO IT

Many babies are fascinated with animals, and animal names are often some of the first words they learn to say. Sit with an infant in your lap and read him a book about baby animals. When you see a picture of a baby animal, point to it or ask him to point to it. Tell him the name of the baby animal, and then ask him what sound the baby animal makes. Make the sound for him, if needed, and ask him to repeat it. Introduce the vocabulary words and sing and chant with the infant.

Modifications for Toddlers and Twos

Read the same books with toddlers and twos, but ask them to name the baby animals and to make the sounds of the baby animals. If the animals' names are next to their pictures, point to their names and say them. Invite the children to turn the pages of the books too.

Expand the Activity

Read touch-and-feel books about baby animals. Invite the baby to touch the animals and talk with him about how the different animals feel, using words such as *soft*, *fuzzy*, *furry*, or *bumpy*.

LEARNING OUTCOMES

SOCIAL-EMOTIONAL DEVELOPMENT
– Sense of self
– Relationships with adults

PHYSICAL DEVELOPMENT
– Fine-motor skills

COGNITIVE DEVELOPMENT
– Memory
– Connecting experiences
– Imitating others
– Following simple directions

LANGUAGE DEVELOPMENT
* Expressive language
* Engaging in print
– Receptive language
– Connecting words with real-world knowledge
– Using language in play

BUILD LANGUAGE SKILLS

Vocabulary

- Baby animal names
- The sounds animals make
  (*peep peep, woof woof,*
  mew mew, baa baa,
  moo moo, and so on)

- Color words
- Farm
- Nest
- Pond

- Run
- Jump
- Baby
- Animal

Questions and Things to Say

"What baby animal is this? This is a baby chick. What do chicks say? Chicks say *peep peep*. Now you say *peep peep*. Yes, baby chicks say *peep peep*. What does the piglet say? The piglet says *oink oink*."

Songs, Chants, and Fingerplays

Song: "Baby Animal Sounds" by Kimberly Bohannon
(Tune: "The Farmer in the Dell")

The baby chick says *peep*.
The baby chick says *peep*.
The baby chick says *peep peep peep*.
The baby chick says *peep*.

Additional verses:
The puppy says *woof woof*.
The kitten says *meow*.
The piglet says *oink oink*.

5

Back to Me, Back to You

MATERIALS

– Small- or medium-size ball

Suggested Books

– *Catch the Ball!* by Eric Carle
– *Elmo's World: Balls!* by Sesame Street
– *Let's Play Ball!* by Serena Romanelli
– *Play Ball!* by Apple Jordan
– *Play Ball!* by Santiago Cohen

HOW TO DO IT

Sit facing an infant who can sit up on her own. Roll the ball to her and watch how she responds. Encourage her to roll the ball back to you. If she is only able to give the ball a slight push, that is fine; simply reach over and take the ball, and then roll it back to her. The back-and-forth rolling of the ball becomes almost like a conversation. Read the suggested books, introduce the vocabulary words, and sing and chant with the infant.

LEARNING OUTCOMES

SOCIAL-EMOTIONAL DEVELOPMENT
– Relationships with adults
– Self-regulation
– Sharing

PHYSICAL DEVELOPMENT
✱ Gross-motor skills
– Perception

COGNITIVE DEVELOPMENT
✱ Cause and effect
– Memory
– Spatial awareness
– Connecting experiences
– Imitating others
– Progression of play
– Following simple directions

LANGUAGE DEVELOPMENT
– Receptive language
– Connecting words with real-world knowledge
– Concept words
– Using language in play

Modifications for Toddlers and Twos

Sit farther apart from toddlers and twos, and take turns rolling the ball back and forth. Invite a second child to join in the game, and then the three of you take turns rolling the ball back and forth.

Expand the Activity

Instead of telling the child to roll the ball back to you, sing a song about what you are doing. For example, use the tune from "Here We Go 'Round the Mulberry Bush" to sing, "This is the way we roll the ball, roll the ball, roll the ball; this is the way we roll the ball early in the morning."

BUILD LANGUAGE SKILLS

Vocabulary

- Roll
- Back
- Me

- You
- Again
- Watch

- Look
- See
- Ball

- Catch
- Stop

Questions and Things to Say

"You caught the ball! Now roll it back to me. I caught the ball, and now I will roll it back to you."

Songs, Chants, and Fingerplays

Song: "This Is the Way" by Jean Barbre
(Tune: "Here We Go 'Round the Mulberry Bush")

This is the way we roll the ball, roll the ball, roll the ball.
This is the way we roll the ball.
Now roll it back to me.

This is the way we bounce the ball, bounce the ball, bounce the ball.
This is the way we bounce the ball.
Now bounce it back to me.

Song: "There's a Ball on the Ground" by Jean Barbre
(Tune: "If You're Happy and You Know It")

There's a ball on the ground, on the ground.
There's a ball on the ground, on the ground.
Let's watch it roll our way,
As it spins and twirls this way.
There's a ball on the ground, on the ground.

There's a ball on the ground, on the ground.
There's a ball on the ground, on the ground.
Let's share it all around,
As we roll it on the ground.
There's a ball on the ground, on the ground.

6

Bubble Babies

MATERIALS

- Bubble solution (store-bought or made from dish soap and water)
- Bubble wand or wire loop

Suggested Books

- *Bubble Bath Baby!* by Libby Ellis
- *Bubble Trouble* by Margaret Mahy
- *Bubbles, Bubbles* by Sesame Street
- *Cinder the Bubble-Blowing Dragon* by Jessica Anderson
- *Clifford Counts Bubbles* by Norman Bridwell

HOW TO DO IT

Lay an infant on her back or sit on the floor with her. Blow the bubbles where she can easily see them but not so close that the bubbles pop near her face and get in her eyes. Watch how she responds. Does she notice the bubbles and follow them with her eyes? Does she make movements to try to catch the bubbles? Does she act surprised when the bubbles pop? Use her responses as cues for how to continue. For example, if she delights in seeing the popping bubbles, show delight yourself by making fun "popping" noises every time a bubble pops. Read the suggested books, introduce the vocabulary words, and sing and chant with the infant.

Modifications for Toddlers and Twos

Hold the bubble wand near the toddler's mouth and ask him to blow into it. If the child is able to hold the bubble wand without putting it in his mouth, let him hold the wand and blow bubbles.

Expand the Activity

Take two or three infants outdoors on a day when there is a slight breeze and repeat the activity. Express excitement and wonder as the bubbles blow away with the wind or pop when they touch a tree branch or shrub.

LEARNING OUTCOMES

SOCIAL-EMOTIONAL DEVELOPMENT
- Sense of self
- Relationships with adults

PHYSICAL DEVELOPMENT
* Perception

COGNITIVE DEVELOPMENT
* Connecting experiences
- Cause and effect
- Memory
- Spatial awareness

LANGUAGE DEVELOPMENT
- Receptive language
- Expressive language
- Connecting words with real-world knowledge
- Concept words

BUILD LANGUAGE SKILLS

Vocabulary

- Bubbles
- Wand
- Pop
- Float
- Big
- Little
- Wet
- Touch
- Blow
- Pretty
- Look

Questions and Things to Say

"Watch as I blow some pretty bubbles. Where are the bubbles going? Pop! The bubble popped when it touched the floor. Watch. Here come some more pretty bubbles!"

Songs, Chants, and Fingerplays

Song: "There's a Bubble" by Kimberly Bohannon
(Tune: "If You're Happy and You Know It")

There's a bubble on my hand, on my hand.
There's a bubble on my hand, on my hand.
There's a bubble on my hand.
There's a bubble on my hand.
There's a bubble on my hand, on my hand.

Additional verses:
There are bubbles in the air.
There's a bubble on my shirt.
There are bubbles everywhere.

Buddy Up!

MATERIALS

Suggested Books

- *Friends at School* by Rochelle Bunnett
- *How Do Dinosaurs Play with Their Friends?*
  by Jane Yolen and Mark Teague
- *That's What a Friend Is* by P. K. Hallinan
- *We Are Best Friends* by Aliki

HOW TO DO IT

It's important to allow babies lots of tummy time. Place two to three babies on their tummies on the floor facing each other. Prop them up using pillows. Sit on the floor next to them and talk to them. You will see older babies reaching for the other children and trying to touch them. Verbalize what you're seeing on their faces and the noises they are making to communicate with each other. Read the suggested books, introduce the vocabulary words, and sing and chant with the infants.

Modifications for Toddlers and Twos

Children love to look at other children's faces. Hold hand mirrors next to toddlers and twos, and talk with them about what they are seeing and the expressions on their faces. Identify the facial and body features of the children sitting next to them. You can do this during free time or mealtime.

Expand the Activity

When children become mobile and can sit up on their own, you'll want to encourage them to play together. Place a toy or object between them, describe the object, and move and rotate it so they can see and play with it. Children will start to learn to take turns.

LEARNING OUTCOMES

SOCIAL-EMOTIONAL DEVELOPMENT
- ★ Relationships with peers
- ★ Empathy
- – Sense of self
- – Personal identity
- – Relationships with adults
- – Caring for others

PHYSICAL DEVELOPMENT
- – Gross-motor skills
- – Fine-motor skills

COGNITIVE DEVELOPMENT
- – Spatial awareness
- – Connecting experiences
- – Imitating others
- – Progression of play

LANGUAGE DEVELOPMENT
- – Receptive language
- – Expressive language
- – Concept words

BUILD LANGUAGE SKILLS

Vocabulary

- Buddy
- Friends
- Smile
- Look
- Laugh
- Talk
- Stomach
- Wiggle

Questions and Things to Say

"Look at Danny smiling at his friend Sophie! You're both kicking your feet and wiggling your bodies. What are you saying to each other? You babies are buddies—that's another word for *friend*."

Songs, Chants, and Fingerplays

Song: "A Buddy Is a Friend" by Kimberly Bohannon
(Tune: "The Farmer in the Dell")

A buddy is a friend.
A buddy is a friend.
A buddy plays and talks with you.
A buddy is a friend.

Chant: "Buddy, Buddy" by Kimberly Bohannon

Buddy, buddy, where are you?
Buddy, buddy, I found you.
Buddy, buddy, I see you!
Buddy, buddy, I love you!

Chant: "Active Buddies" by Kimberly Bohannon

Buddy, buddy, laugh with me.
Buddy, buddy, play with me.
Buddy, buddy, smile with me.
Buddy, buddy, wiggle with me.

8

Come to Me

MATERIALS

– Small toys or objects that will interest an infant, such as noise-making or brightly colored toys

Suggested Books

– *Caillou Moves Around* by Christine L'Heureux
– *First Steps* by Lee Wardlaw
– *I Can* by Helen Oxenbury
– *Ready, Set, Walk!* by Warner Brothers
– *Wiggle and Move* by Sanja Rescek

HOW TO DO IT

To encourage an infant who is not yet crawling to crawl to you, begin by laying him on his tummy.
Sit a short distance away from him and set the toy next to you. Say his name and invite him to crawl to you and get the toy. Be sure to reinforce his efforts as he attempts to crawl. If he reaches you, give him the toy and encourage him to explore it. Read the suggested books, introduce the vocabulary words, and sing and chant with the infant.

LEARNING OUTCOMES

SOCIAL-EMOTIONAL DEVELOPMENT
– Sense of self
– Personal identity

PHYSICAL DEVELOPMENT
✴ Gross-motor skills
– Perception

COGNITIVE DEVELOPMENT
✴ Spatial awareness
– Cause and effect
– Following simple directions

LANGUAGE DEVELOPMENT
– Receptive language
– Concept words

Modifications for Toddlers and Twos

Encourage a toddler who is not yet walking to walk to you. Begin by having her stand next to something she is familiar with for support. Sit or kneel a short distance from her and set the toy next to you. Say her name and invite her to walk to you and pick up the toy. If she is successful, give her the toy and encourage her to hold and explore it.

Expand the Activity

After an infant has mastered crawling a short distance, increase the distance and invite him to crawl to you from farther away.

BUILD LANGUAGE SKILLS

Vocabulary

- Crawl
- Come
- Here
- Close
- Closer
- Almost
- Farther
- Get
- Me
- Name of toy or object
- Move
- Arms
- Legs
- Hands

Questions and Things to Say

"Jack, I have a shaker you might like to hold and shake. I will put it right here next to me. See if you can crawl on your tummy all the way over here and get this shaker. You moved your arm, and then you moved your leg. You are getting closer and closer to the shaker."

Songs, Chants, and Fingerplays

Song: "Shake the Toy" by Jean Barbre
(Tune: "Bingo")

I have a toy that you can see
So come this way toward me.
Shake, shake, shake the toy,
Shake, shake, shake the toy,
Shake, shake, shake the toy,
And come this way toward me.

(Choose a rattle, soft toy, or brightly colored object to shake as you sing this song.)

Additional verses:
Replace "walk" with "crawl" as appropriate.

9

Do You Hear What I Hear?

MATERIALS

Suggested Books

- *Baby Sounds: A Baby-Sized Introduction to Sounds We Hear Everyday* by Joy Allen
- *Baby's First Sounds* by Hinkler Books
- *Boom Boom, Beep Beep, Roar! My Sounds Book* by David Diehl
- *Polar Bear, Polar Bear, What Do You Hear?* by Bill Martin Jr. and Eric Carle
- *The Sounds around Town* by Maria Carluccio
- *What's That Noise?* by Sally Rippin

HOW TO DO IT

Outdoor environments offer endless opportunities for awakening the senses. Take an infant outdoors to listen for sounds, such as cars, trucks, children playing, people working, animals, birds, and the wind blowing through trees. Stop and name the sound you hear. Point in the direction of the sound or to the thing making the sound. See if the infant follows with his eyes. Spend time listening to each sound for several minutes. Then listen for a new sound. Read the suggested books, introduce the vocabulary words, and sing and chant with the infant.

Modifications for Toddlers and Twos

Ask the child to listen for a sound and name it. If you can't see what is making the sound, search for its source together.

Expand the Activity

Imitate the sounds you hear, such as a barking dog or rumbling truck. Tell the infant, "I hear a dog barking: *Woof! Woof!*" Encourage the infant to make the sound too. "Let's make the sound of the barking dog together: *Woof! Woof!*"

LEARNING OUTCOMES

SOCIAL-EMOTIONAL DEVELOPMENT
- Sense of self
- Relationships with adults

PHYSICAL DEVELOPMENT
- Perception

COGNITIVE DEVELOPMENT
- ★ Memory
- Connecting experiences
- Imitating others
- Following simple directions

LANGUAGE DEVELOPMENT
- ★ Concept words
- Receptive language
- Expressive language
- Connecting words with real-world knowledge
- Using language in play

BUILD LANGUAGE SKILLS

Vocabulary

- Hear
- Ears
- What
- Sound

- Listen
- Shhh
- Loud
- Noisy

- Quiet
- Whisper
- Soft

- Names of other
  things you hear

Questions and Things to Say

"Do you hear what I hear? What is that sound? Where is it coming from? Oh! I see what is making that sound. It's a noisy bird up in that tree. Do you see the bird? Do you hear the bird saying *tweet, tweet, tweet*?"

Songs, Chants, and Fingerplays

Song: "Put on Your Listening Ears" by Kimberly Bohannon
(Tune: "Hokey Pokey")

Put your listening ears on.
Put your listening ears on.
Put your listening ears on.
And listen all around.
Let's stand nice and quiet
As we listen for the sounds.
Now tell me the sounds you hear.

Expressing Emotions

MATERIALS

– Books with storylines that may elicit a variety of emotional responses, such as a book in which someone is looking for something or needs something (for example, *Are You My Mother?* by P. D. Eastman)

Suggested Books

– *Bear Feels Scared* by Karma Wilson
– *Feelings to Share* by Todd and Peggy Snow
– *Gossie* by Oliver Dunrea
– *The Pigeon Has Feelings, Too!* by Mo Willems
– *What's Wrong, Little Pookie?* by Sandra Boynton

HOW TO DO IT

Infants demonstrate an awareness of others' feelings by reacting to their emotional expressions. Select a book, such as one suggested above, and read it to an infant. As you read, use your voice to express emotions, such as concern, bewilderment, surprise, and happiness—whatever emotion is appropriate. Introduce the vocabulary words and sing and chant with the infant.

Modifications for Toddlers and Twos

Sit with a small group of toddlers and twos and read a similar type of book, such as *Is Your Mama a Llama?* by Deborah Guarino. More so than infants, toddlers and twos may become caught up in the emotions of the book and express themselves through words such as "Uh-oh!" or clap their hands at a happy ending.

Expand the Activity

Notice when children display emotions throughout the day and call the infants' attention to them, such as when children are laughing. Ask the infants what they hear and see the other children doing. Explain, "They are laughing and smiling because the book Debbie is reading is so funny. Look at them laughing and smiling."

LEARNING OUTCOMES

SOCIAL-EMOTIONAL DEVELOPMENT
✱ Empathy
– Relationships with adults
– Relationships with peers
– Caring for others

PHYSICAL DEVELOPMENT
– Perception

COGNITIVE DEVELOPMENT
– Cause and effect
– Memory
– Connecting experiences

LANGUAGE DEVELOPMENT
✱ Communicating needs
– Receptive language
– Expressive language
– Connecting words with real-world knowledge
– Concept words
– Engaging in print

BUILD LANGUAGE SKILLS

Vocabulary

- Feeling
- Happy
- Laughing

- Funny
- Sad
- Crying

- Tears
- Looking
- Surprised

- Care
- Want

Questions and Things to Say

"What is the baby bird looking for? He needs his mommy. He is sad. Where is his mommy? Will he find his mommy?"

Songs, Chants, and Fingerplays

Song: "We Love Mommy"
by Jean Barbre
(Tune: "Frère Jacques")

We love Mommy.
We love Mommy.
Yes, we do.
Yes, we do.
It's okay to miss her.
It's okay to miss her.
I love you.
I love you.

Additional Verses:
Replace "Mommy" with "Daddy" and other terms of endearment children and families use.

Here I Come

MATERIALS

Suggested Books

- *Baby Happy, Baby Sad* by Leslie Patricelli
- *Hug* by Jez Alborough
- *I Love You Through and Through*
  by Bernadette Rossetti-Shustak
- *Wah! Wah! A Backpack Baby Story*
  by Miriam Cohen
- *What Shall We Do with the Boo-Hoo Baby?*
  by Cressida Cowell

HOW TO DO IT

Responding to an infant's needs in a timely and caring manner helps establish the security and trust that form the foundation for her healthy growth and development. Pay close attention to times when she is upset or scared. Even if you can't respond to her immediately, say her name to reassure her and tell her you will be there very soon. Read the suggested books, introduce the vocabulary words, and sing and chant with the infant.

Modifications for Toddlers and Twos

Toddlers and twos still need your attention and reassurance when they are upset, but they may be quieted easier because their language and communication skills (both receptive and expressive) are more advanced. They have a better understanding of what you tell them and, as important, can often tell you what is wrong or what they need. Try to keep a short dialogue going until you can go to the child.

Expand the Activity

Playing soft music or singing quiet songs while you perform routine tasks such as diaper-changing can sooth infants who are waiting for your attention and care.

LEARNING OUTCOMES

SOCIAL-EMOTIONAL DEVELOPMENT
- ✱ Relationships with adults
- Sense of self
- Personal identity
- Self-regulation

PHYSICAL DEVELOPMENT
- Perception

COGNITIVE DEVELOPMENT
- Cause and effect
- Memory
- Spatial awareness
- Connecting experiences

LANGUAGE DEVELOPMENT
- ✱ Communicating needs
- Receptive language
- Expressive language
- Connecting words with real-world knowledge
- Concept words

BUILD LANGUAGE SKILLS

Vocabulary

- Here I come
- I am coming
- Your turn
- I hear you
- I see you
- You are next

Questions and Things to Say

"I hear you, Adam. As soon as I finish with Jake, I will be there. Here I come!" "Look what I have for you, Moira. I have your bottle. Let's sit together in this chair and I will give you your bottle."

Songs, Chants, and Fingerplays

Song: "Here I Come" by Jean Barbre
(Tune: "Row, Row, Row Your Boat")

Here, here, here I come.
I'm walking right to you.
Here I come to have some fun
To laugh and play with you.

Song: "I Hear You" by Kimberly Bohannon
(Tune: "You Are My Sunshine")

I hear you, Adam.
I hear you, Adam.
And I will be there
To help you soon.
Yes, I am coming,
And I will help you.
Now, I'm here,
And it's time to feed you.

Additional verses:
Replace "Adam" with names of children in your care. Replace "time to feed you" with other moments in your daily routine, such as "time to hold you" or "time to play with you."

How Many?

MATERIALS

– Several of the same small infant toy (such as a rubber or squeaky toy) or several of the same child-safe object (such as a plastic cup)

Suggested Books

– *Hands Off! They're Mine! A Book About Sharing* by Mary Packard
– *I Am Sharing* by Mercer Mayer
– *Let's Share* by P. K. Hallinan
– *Mine! A Sesame Street Book About Sharing* by Linda Hayward
– *Sharing Time* by Elizabeth Verdick

HOW TO DO IT

Young children develop the capacity to share over time, but you can help set the stage for sharing through simple activities in which all children have similar toys and by talking about the toys together. With another caregiver, gather three or four infants and sit with them on your laps or in front of you on the floor. Give each infant one toy to hold or place one toy on the floor in front of each infant. Talk about how each of them has one toy and how the toys are similar. Count the toys aloud and tell the babies how many toys they each have and how many toys there are altogether. Read the suggested books, introduce the vocabulary words, and sing and chant with the infants.

Modifications for Toddlers and Twos

Give toddlers and twos one or two different types of toys. Encourage them to identify or name the toys and talk about how the toys are the same and different. For example, you might say, "What toy does Jasmine have? Yes, Jasmine has a toy car too. Does Jasmine's car make a noise like Angelo's car?"

LEARNING OUTCOMES

SOCIAL-EMOTIONAL DEVELOPMENT
✶ Sharing
– Sense of self
– Personal identity
– Relationships with peers
– Self-regulation
– Empathy

PHYSICAL DEVELOPMENT
– Fine-motor skills

COGNITIVE DEVELOPMENT
✶ Number awareness
– Connecting experiences
– Imitating others
– Progression of play
– Following simple directions

LANGUAGE DEVELOPMENT
– Receptive language
– Expressive language
– Connecting words with real-world knowledge
– Concept words
– Using language in play

Expand the Activity

Give infants toys that do the same thing, such as balls that roll across the floor. Instead of talking about how the toys look the same or have similar physical qualities, talk about what the toys do that is the same. For example, do the toys make noise? Do they bounce when dropped? Do they roll across the floor? Encourage the children to test the toys to see if they do the same thing; for example, say, "Let's see if your ball rolls across the floor too."

BUILD LANGUAGE SKILLS

Vocabulary

- Name of toy
- Your toy
- His/her toy
- Yours
- His
- Hers
- Mine
- Same toy
- One
- Two
- Three
- Four
- Five
- Share
- Please
- Thank you
- Physical characteristics of toys (such as their color, shape, and texture)

Questions and Things to Say

"Look. Eli has a fish. Who else has a fish? Where is your fish, Emma? Emma has a fish just like Eli's."

Songs, Chants, and Fingerplays

Song: "We Can Share"
by Kimberly Bohannon
(Tune: "The Farmer in the Dell")

We can share our toys.
We can share our toys.
We take turns and use new words.
Yes, we can share our toys.

Chant: "Same Game"
by Kimberly Bohannon

It's time to find
What is the same.
Let's start with this.
What is its name?
"It's a toy car."

(Ask questions about the toy. Then find an object that is similar and discuss how it is similar to and different from the toy.)

Additional verses:
Replace "toy car" with other objects in the environment.

Musical Babies

MATERIALS

- CD player or MP3 player
- CD or MP3 files of short children's songs (or other short songs babies might enjoy)

Suggested Books

- *Baby Mozart: Music Is Everywhere* by Julie Aigner-Clark
- *Elmo's World: Music!* by Random House
- *Music: Discovering Musical Horizons* by Brainy Baby Company
- *Music Play* by H. A. Rey
- *Pat the Bunny: Shake, Shake, Bunny* by Golden Books

HOW TO DO IT

Music is an important part of early childhood programs because it can be used to enhance children's learning across all developmental domains—not to mention that most babies enjoy listening and moving to music. This game is similar to Musical Chairs. While the music plays, carry and move with the infant around the room. When the music stops, stop moving. When the music starts again, resume moving. The more enthusiastic you are when stopping and starting, the more likely the baby will engage in the game as well. Read the suggested books, introduce the vocabulary words, and sing and chant with the infant.

Modifications for Toddlers and Twos

Toddlers and twos may be able to play the game more like traditional Musical Chairs. When you start the music, have the children move around the play area any way they wish. When you stop the music, have the children sit on the floor.

LEARNING OUTCOMES

SOCIAL-EMOTIONAL DEVELOPMENT
* Relationships with peers
- Sense of self
- Relationships with adults

PHYSICAL DEVELOPMENT
- Gross-motor skills

COGNITIVE DEVELOPMENT
- Cause and effect
- Memory
- Spatial awareness
- Connecting experiences
- Progression of play
- Following simple directions

LANGUAGE DEVELOPMENT
* Engaging in music, rhythm, and rhyme
- Receptive language
- Expressive language
- Using language in play

Expand the Activity

Invite other caregivers and babies to join in the game. You and the other caregivers move around the space singing songs. Stop moving when you stop singing. Again, showing enthusiasm and changing the way you move (walk quickly, walk slowly, wiggle around, or dance) may engage the babies in the game even more.

BUILD LANGUAGE SKILLS

Vocabulary

- Sing
- Song
- Music
- Stop
- Go
- Move
- Play
- Dance
- Walk
- Quickly
- Slowly

Questions and Things to Say

"Let's listen to some music. While the music plays, we will walk around the room, but when the music stops, we must stop too. Oh! I hear music, so we need to get moving! Oh, oh! The music stopped, so we must stop too."

Songs, Chants, and Fingerplays

Song: "Stop and Go" by Kimberly Bohannon
(Tune: "This Old Man")

Stop and go.
Stop and go.
Let's walk fast.
Now, let's walk slow.
When the music starts,
We'll walk around the room.
When it stops,
Then we'll stop too.

My Kind of Play

MATERIALS

– Toys or objects that move, change shape, or can be taken apart into pieces that are not too small

Suggested Books

– *Baby Playtime!* By DK Publishing
– *Baby's First Toys* by Hinkler Books
– *Playtime* by Claire Belmont
– *Playtime* by Roger Priddy
– *Playtime: Push, Pull, and Play* by Emma Damon
– *Pop-up Peekaboo! Playtime* by DK Publishing

HOW TO DO IT

Children's play progresses from solitary play to cooperative play. Infants typically engage in solitary play, which is characterized by simple, repetitive motor movements and may or may not involve toys or other objects. For this activity, give an infant a toy or an object. Watch as she explores something by squishing it, rolling it, or shaking it over and over. Or watch as she waves her fingers in front of her face, fascinated not only with the movement but with her ability to cause the movement. Read the suggested books, introduce the vocabulary words, and sing and chant with the infant.

Modifications for Toddlers and Twos

The movements of most toddlers and twos are more refined and their attention spans are a bit longer. You may be surprised by how long a toddler can repeat the same action before moving on to something new.

Expand the Activity

Join in the play by doing what the infant is doing. Talk with her about what you both are doing.

LEARNING OUTCOMES

SOCIAL-EMOTIONAL DEVELOPMENT
✳ Sense of self
– Personal identity

PHYSICAL DEVELOPMENT
– Perception
– Fine-motor skills

COGNITIVE DEVELOPMENT
✳ Cause and effect
– Memory
– Spatial awareness
– Connecting experiences

LANGUAGE DEVELOPMENT
– Receptive language
– Expressive language
– Connecting words with real-world knowledge
– Concept words

BUILD LANGUAGE SKILLS

Vocabulary

Words that describe what the infant is doing with the toy or object:

- Roll
- Push
- Pull
- Tap

- Squish
- Shake
- Drop
- Crunch

- Tear
- Hold

Questions and Things to Say

"What are you holding? You are holding a piece of paper. The paper makes a noise: *crunch, crunch, crunch.* You are crunching the piece of paper."

Songs, Chants, and Fingerplays

Song: "We Are Playing" by Jean Barbre
(Tune: "London Bridge Is Falling Down")

Watch the children learn and grow,
Learn and grow,
Learn and grow.
Watch the children learn and grow.
We are playing.
Hear their laughter, see their smiles,
See their smiles,
See their smiles.
Hear their laughter, see their smiles.
We are playing.

15

Peekaboo

MATERIALS

Suggested Books

- *Eyes, Nose, Fingers, and Toes: A First Book All About You* by Judy Hindley
- *Hello! Good-bye!* by Aliki
- *My Hands* by Aliki
- *Where Is My Friend?* by Simms Taback

HOW TO DO IT

Babies love to play peekaboo. Just cover your face with your hands, and watch the delight on the child's face as you pull your hands away. Babies are learning that although they can't see you, they know you're still there. Doing so helps strengthen their memory skills and their ability to control their environment. Read the suggested books, introduce the vocabulary words, and sing and chant with the infant.

Modifications for Toddlers and Twos

Two-year-olds will want to be the ones who hide behind their hands and play peekaboo with you.

Expand the Activity

Select a windup musical toy. Demonstrate how to wind it up, and let the children listen to the sound it makes. Hide the toy in an easy-to-find location, and then wind it. Invite the children to listen to the sound of the music and find the hidden toy. Children may need some assistance at first, but they will quickly learn how to find the toy and then hide it for you.

LEARNING OUTCOMES

SOCIAL-EMOTIONAL DEVELOPMENT
- ✱ Sense of self
- Personal identity
- Relationships with adults
- Caring for others

PHYSICAL DEVELOPMENT
- Fine-motor skills

COGNITIVE DEVELOPMENT
- ✱ Cause and effect
- Memory
- Connecting experiences
- Imitating others
- Progression of play

LANGUAGE DEVELOPMENT
- Receptive language
- Expressive language
- Engaging in music, rhythm, and rhyme
- Using language in play

BUILD LANGUAGE SKILLS

Vocabulary

- Peekaboo
- I
- See
- Face
- Hands
- Hide
- You

Questions and Things to Say

"I'm going to hide behind my hands. Can you see me? Now you can! Where is the baby? Where is the teacher?"

Songs, Chants, and Fingerplays

Song: "Where Are You?" by Kimberly Bohannon
(Tune: "Frère Jacques")

Where are you?
Where are you?
Peekaboo,
Peekaboo,
I'm so glad to see you.
I'm so glad to see you.
I love you.
I love you.

Chant: "Peekaboo" by Kimberly Bohannon

Peekaboo.
Peekaboo.
I see you.
Peekaboo.
Peekaboo.
I love you.

Rhyme with Me

MATERIALS

– Books containing familiar children's rhymes, fingerplays, and songs (if needed)

Suggested Books

– *A Children's Treasury of Nursery Rhymes* by Linda Bleck
– *A Children's Treasury of Songs* by Linda Bleck
– *Chicka Chicka Boom Boom* by Bill Martin Jr. and John Archambault
– *Clare Beaton's Bedtime Rhymes* by Clare Beaton
– *Fingerplays and Songs for the Very Young* by Random House
– *Pat-a-Cake! Nursery Rhymes* by Annie Kubler

LEARNING OUTCOMES

SOCIAL-EMOTIONAL DEVELOPMENT
– Sense of self
– Personal identity
– Relationships with adults

COGNITIVE DEVELOPMENT
– Memory
– Connecting experiences
– Number awareness
– Imitating others
– Progression of play
– Following simple directions

LANGUAGE DEVELOPMENT
∗ Engaging in music, rhythm, and rhyme
∗ Using language in play
– Receptive language
– Expressive language

HOW TO DO IT

Select a rhyme, fingerplay, or song you think might interest an infant; use the song or one of the fingerplays suggested below or pick one of your own favorites. Hold him on your lap or sit next to him on the floor. Begin the song, being sure to show enthusiasm as you sing and as you walk the spider up the infant's arm or leg. Repeat the song several times a day. Young children take comfort in activities that are repeated, and in no time, the infant will begin to show recognition and delight whenever you begin the familiar song. Read the suggested books and introduce the vocabulary words to the infant.

Modifications for Toddlers and Twos

Children will begin performing with you or will want to perform the song or fingerplay themselves. Smile and play along, commenting on how the spider is tickling you as it makes its way up your arm or leg.

Expand the Activity

Consider singing certain songs or saying certain rhymes while performing daily routines. Not only will the infant enjoy hearing them again, but he may also come to associate them with specific activities such as diapering or having his face and hands washed after a meal. You will know he has made this connection when you see him anticipating what comes next, such as looking toward the changing table or the sink.

BUILD LANGUAGE SKILLS

Vocabulary

Words from the rhyme, song, or fingerplay you choose. In the case of "Itsy, Bitsy Spider," these may include the following:

- Itsy
- Bitsy
- Spider
- Climbed
- Up
- Waterspout
- Down
- Rain
- Washed
- Sun
- Dried
- Again

Questions and Things to Say

"I'd like to tell you about a little spider who got caught in the rain. Let's pretend my fingers are the spider. Watch as I sing the song and the spider climbs up the waterspout. What happens when the rain comes down? The little spider gets washed back down, like this—*whoosh*!"

Songs, Chants, and Fingerplays

Song: "It's Time" by Kimberly Bohannon
(Tune: "Head, Shoulders, Knees, and Toes")

It's time to wash our faces and hands,
Faces and hands.
It's time to wash our faces and hands,
Faces and hands.
It's time to get towels and some soap.
It's time to wash our faces and hands.
Splash! Splash!

Fingerplay: "Itsy, Bitsy Spider" (traditional)
Fingerplay: "Pat-a-Cake!" (traditional)
Fingerplay: "Hickory Dickory Dock" (traditional)

Touch-It Tubs

MATERIALS

– Plastic tubs, such as small washtubs
– A variety of items that are appropriate and safe for infants to explore with their hands and mouths:
  › Small toys with different textures
  › Fabric samples with different textures (burlap, velvet, faux fur, fleece)
  › Clean lids from baby-food jars or frozen juice cans
  › Items that make noise when banged together, such as measuring cups and spoons

Suggested Books

– *Baby Touch and Feel 1, 2, 3* by DK Publishing
– *Baby Touch and Feel Farm* by DK Publishing
– *Pooh's Touch and Feel Visit* by A. A. Milne
– *Touch and Feel Adventure: Discovering Colors and Textures* by Alexis Barad-Cutler
– *Whose Back Is Bumpy?* by Kate Davis

LEARNING OUTCOMES

SOCIAL–EMOTIONAL DEVELOPMENT
– Sense of self
– Personal identity
– Relationships with peers
– Sharing

PHYSICAL DEVELOPMENT
* Fine-motor skills
– Perception

COGNITIVE DEVELOPMENT
* Connecting experiences
– Cause and effect
– Spatial awareness

LANGUAGE DEVELOPMENT
– Receptive language
– Expressive language
– Connecting words with real-world knowledge
– Concept words
– Using language in play

HOW TO DO IT

Place the items in the tubs. Place the tubs in an area where infants can explore what's inside the tubs, either by sitting next to you for support or by sitting up independently. For infants who enjoy exploring on their tummies, place the items on the floor in front of them, either at a distance (to encourage crawling) or close enough for them to reach out and grasp. Read the suggested books, introduce the vocabulary words, and sing and chant with the infants.

Modifications for Toddlers and Twos

Add sand to the tubs to encourage activities such as scooping and pouring.

Expand the Activity

Take the tubs outdoors and fill them with safe, natural items that infants can explore with their hands and mouths.

BUILD LANGUAGE SKILLS

Vocabulary

- Touch
- Taste
- Soft
- Bumpy
- Smooth

- Fuzzy
- Squishy
- Shiny
- Cold
- Warm

- Hand
- Fingers
- Hold
- Noise
- Hear

- Bang
- Tub

Questions and Things to Say

"You have a funny ball with bumps all over it. Feel the bumps? What happens when you squeeze the ball? Oh! It makes a noise!"

Songs, Chants, and Fingerplays

Song: "What's in the Tub?" by Jean Barbre
(Tune: "The More We Get Together")

What's in the tub, the tub, the tub?
What's in the tub? Come and see.
Soft things and hard things,
Round things and square things,
What's in the tub, the tub, the tub?
What's in the tub? Come and see.

18

Water Babies

MATERIALS

- Water
- One or two large towels
- Small tub or container with sides
- Small washcloths
- Small plastic cups for scooping and pouring

Suggested Books

- *Baby Faces: Splash!* Roberta Grobel Intrater
- *Baby's World Touch and Explore: Splish-Splash*
  by DK Publishing
- *Board Buddies: Swim!* by Marilyn Brigham
- *Splash!* by Flora McDonnell
- *Splash!* by Sarah Garland

HOW TO DO IT

In this activity, you and the infant may get a bit
wet, so be sure to prepare accordingly. Also, make
sure the washcloths are clean, because the infant
may put the washcloth in his mouth. Place a
towel on the floor. Pour no more than a half inch
of water in the tub and set the tub and the wash-
cloths on the towel. Sit on the towel with the infant in front of you facing the tub. Show
him a dry washcloth and invite him to feel it. Then have him drop it in the tub of water
(drop the washcloth in the water for him, if needed). Remove the washcloth and have him
feel the wet washcloth. Ring out the washcloth and have him hold it again. Encourage ex-
perimentation with the water in the tub by having the infant place his hand in the water or
by scooping and pouring water from a plastic cup. Read the suggested books, introduce the
vocabulary words, and sing and chant with the infant.

Modifications for Toddlers and Twos

Have children wash plastic baby dolls or other toys in the water with the washcloths.

LEARNING OUTCOMES

SOCIAL-EMOTIONAL DEVELOPMENT
- Sense of self
- Personal identity

PHYSICAL DEVELOPMENT
- Perception
- Gross-motor skills
- Fine-motor skills

COGNITIVE DEVELOPMENT
✱ Cause and effect
- Spatial awareness
- Connecting experiences
- Imitating others
- Progression of play
- Following simple directions

LANGUAGE DEVELOPMENT
✱ Concept words
- Receptive language
- Expressive language
- Communicating needs
- Connecting words with
  real-world knowledge
- Using language in play

Expand the Activity

Take the activity outdoors on a warm, sunny day. Trickle water on the infant's legs or dip her fingers and toes in the water to expand the sensory experience.

BUILD LANGUAGE SKILLS

Vocabulary

- Wet
- Dry
- Water
- Washcloth
- Twist

- Squeeze
- Clean
- Wash
- Drop
- Tub

- Cool
- Taste
- Splash

Questions and Things to Say

"This washcloth is dry now. Feel it. It is dry. What will happen when you drop the washcloth in the water? Is it dry now? No, the washcloth is wet now. It is full of water. When I squeeze the washcloth, look what happens. Water comes out! Splash! Splash!"

Songs, Chants, and Fingerplays

Song: "Water Dripping" by Jean Barbre
(Tune: "Frère Jacques")

Water dripping,
Water dripping,
Watch it fall,
Watch it fall.
Watch the water dripping.
Watch the water dripping.
Watch it fall.
Watch it fall.
Squeeze the washcloth.
Squeeze the washcloth.
Ring it out.
Ring it out.
Watch the water dripping.
Watch the water dripping.
Ring it out.
Ring it out.

What Do You See?

MATERIALS

Suggested Books

- *101 First Words at Home* by Hinkler Studios
- *First 100 Words* by Roger Priddy
- *Flaptastic First Words* by DK Publishing
- *My Big Animal Book* by Roger Priddy
- *Things That Move* by Jo Litchfield
- *Very First Words* by Felicity Brooks

HOW TO DO IT

Sit with the infant on your lap (indoors or outdoors). Point to things in the environment. Slowly call his attention to the things he is most likely to notice, such as brightly colored objects or things that are making a noise. Name the things you point to and talk about them. Read the suggested books, introduce the vocabulary words, and sing and chant with the infant.

Modifications for Toddlers and Twos

After pointing to and naming something, ask the children to tell you what they see. If the thing you point to makes a noise, such as a dog or cat, ask the children what the animal "says" (that is, what noise the animal makes).

Expand the Activity

Hold the baby and walk around an entire area. Stop before pointing to and naming an object.

LEARNING OUTCOMES

SOCIAL-EMOTIONAL DEVELOPMENT
- Personal identity
- Relationships with adults

PHYSICAL DEVELOPMENT
- Perception

COGNITIVE DEVELOPMENT
- Memory
- Spatial awareness
- Connecting experiences
- Following simple directions

LANGUAGE DEVELOPMENT
- ✴ Receptive language
- ✴ Connecting words with real-world knowledge

BUILD LANGUAGE SKILLS

Vocabulary

- What
- Where
- Look
- See
- There
- This

- Who
- Table
- Chair
- Rug
- Window
- Door

- Cup
- Color words
- Other things you see in the room
- Tree
- Bush

- Grass
- Bird
- Sky
- Cloud
- Other things you see outdoors

Questions and Things to Say

"What is this? This is a chair. Who is sitting in the chair? Charlie is sitting in the chair." "What do you see over there? That's a big tree. The tree has colored leaves that have fallen on the grass."

Songs, Chants, and Fingerplays

Song: "What Do You See?" by Kimberly Bohannon
(Tune: "London Bridge Is Falling Down")

Look at this! What do you see?
What do you see?
What do you see?
Look at this! What do you see?
It's a red ball.

Additional verses:
Replace "red ball" with other objects in the environment (such as a truck, a bird, or a tree).

What's in the Shoe Box?

MATERIALS

- Small shoe boxes with lids
- Small toys or items that will fit inside the shoe boxes (such as measuring cups and spoons)
- Rattles
- Soft animals

Suggested Books

- *Look!* by Annie Kubler
- *What Does Baby See?* by Begin Smart Books
- *What's in Grandma's Grocery Bag?* by Hui-Mei Pan
- *What's in the Box?* by Richard Powell
- *What's in the Toy Box?* by Dawn Bentley

HOW TO DO IT

Place the items in the shoe boxes and cover them with the lids. Sit behind the infant who is not yet sitting on her own to lend support, or sit next to an infant who can sit on her own. Place the shoe boxes on the floor in front of the infant. Pick up one of the shoe boxes, shake it, and ask the infant what might be inside. Encourage her to remove the lid and look inside. If the infant can't remove the lid, slowly remove it for her. Have the infant look inside. What does she see? Repeat the activity with a different box or place a different object in the same box. Read the suggested books, introduce the vocabulary words, and sing and chant with the infant.

Modifications for Toddlers and Twos

Instead of shoe boxes, place different small items or toys beneath large stacking cups. Ask the children to guess what is under a cup. Then have a child pick up the cup to see what is under it. Repeat this action with the other cups. Extend the game by asking the children to place things beneath the cups for you to find.

LEARNING OUTCOMES

SOCIAL-EMOTIONAL DEVELOPMENT
- Sense of self

PHYSICAL DEVELOPMENT
- ✱ Fine-motor skills
- Perception

COGNITIVE DEVELOPMENT
- ✱ Memory
- Cause and effect
- Spatial awareness
- Connecting experiences
- Number awareness
- Following simple directions

LANGUAGE DEVELOPMENT
- Receptive language
- Expressive language
- Connecting words with real-world knowledge
- Concept words
- Using language in play

Expand the Activity

Gather more small items or toys that will fit inside the shoe boxes. Invite the infant to fill the boxes with the items, place the lids on the boxes, and then remove the lids and the items again. Count them as they are removed to introduce the concept of numbers and counting.

BUILD LANGUAGE SKILLS

Vocabulary

– What	– Find	– Close	– Cover
– In	– Something	– Shoe box	– Hide
– Inside	– Out	– Box	
– Look	– Open	– Lid	

Questions and Things to Say

"There is something in this box. What is it? Let's open the lid and see what is in the box. Try to open the lid, Maddie. What do you see? Oh! It's a cup! Take the cup out of the box. Now put the cup back in the box. Try to put the lid back on the box."

Songs, Chants, and Fingerplays

Song: "Shake, Shake, Shake the Box" by Jean Barbre
(Tune: "Row, Row, Row Your Boat")

Shake, shake, shake the box.
Shake it up and down.
Lift the lid and look inside
To see what you have found.

Song: "Oh, There's Something in the Box" by Jean Barbre
(Tune: "If You're Happy and You Know It")

Oh, there's something in the box, in the box.
Oh, there's something in the box, in the box.
When we open up our eyes,
We'll see a big surprise.
Oh, there's something in the box, in the box.

Where Did It Go?

MATERIALS

– Small blanket or towel
– Brightly colored toy or a favorite toy

Suggested Books

– *Peek-a-Baby* by Karen Katz
– *Peek-a-Boo!* by Roberta Grobel Intrater
– *Peekaboo Baby* by Sebastien Braun
– *Playtime Peekaboo!* by DK Publishing
– *Where's Ellie?* by Salina Yoon

HOW TO DO IT

Most young infants have not developed the concept of object permanence, the idea that an object is still there even though they can't see it. After getting a baby's attention, hide a toy beneath a blanket. Pull back the blanket to reveal the toy and act surprised. Repeat this action for as long as she is interested. Hold the baby on your lap and read peekaboo books or books in which things are hidden. Older infants may also enjoy lifting books with flaps to find hidden things. Read the suggested books, introduce the vocabulary words, and sing and chant with the infant.

Modifications for Toddlers and Twos

Play the same game with a toddler, but after you hide the toy, ask her to find it for you.

Expand the Activity

Have the children hide the toy from you and try to find it. Act surprised both when you find the toy and when the toy "disappears."

LEARNING OUTCOMES

SOCIAL-EMOTIONAL DEVELOPMENT
– Relationships with adults

PHYSICAL DEVELOPMENT
✳ Perception

COGNITIVE DEVELOPMENT
✳ Spatial awareness
– Cause and effect
– Memory
– Connecting experiences
– Imitating others

LANGUAGE DEVELOPMENT
– Receptive language
– Connecting words with real-world knowledge
– Concept words
– Using language in play

BUILD LANGUAGE SKILLS

Vocabulary

- Where
- Here
- Under
- Look
- Hiding
- Blanket
- Found

Questions and Things to Say

"Where is your bear? Where did it go? Should I look under the blanket? Oh! Here it is! The silly bear was hiding under your blanket. Here is your bear. Give your bear a big hug."

Songs, Chants, and Fingerplays

Song: "Something's Hiding" by Kimberly Bohannon
(Tune: "Frère Jacques")

Something's hiding.
Something's hiding.
Where is it?
Where is it?
It's under the blanket.
It's under the blanket.
What is it?
What is it?

Chant: "I See Something" by Kimberly Bohannon

I see something.
What will it be?
I see something.
Let's check and see.

Who Is This?

MATERIALS

- Several photographs of each infant (or photocopies of photographs)
- Masking tape (if desired)

Suggested Books

- *Baby Face: A Mirror Book* by Gwynne L. Isaacs and Evelyn Clarke Mott
- *Hello Baby: A Black and White Mirror Book* by Roger Priddy
- *I See Me!* by Julie Aigner-Clark
- *I See Me!* by Pegi Deitz Shea
- *Who's That Baby?* by Susan Amerikaner

HOW TO DO IT

During the first six months of life, infants show an increasing awareness of self as distinct from other people and objects. Place or tape several photographs of the infant around the room in plain view, such as on a cupboard, shelf, or mirror near the cribs. If the baby is able to hold up her head, place several photographs where she can see them when she is on her tummy on the floor. Carry the infant around the room and look for her photographs together, being sure to express excitement and delight when you locate her photo. Read the suggested books, introduce the vocabulary words, and sing and chant with the infant.

Modifications for Toddlers and Twos

Tape photographs of each child around the room in plain view. Then walk around the room while each child locates her own photos or the photos of other children. After all of the photos have been found, collect the photos and gather the children together. Discuss the photos by asking questions such as, "Who is this a picture of? Yes, it's a picture of Isaac. Isaac is wearing his favorite red sweater."

LEARNING OUTCOMES

SOCIAL-EMOTIONAL DEVELOPMENT
* Personal identity
- Sense of self

PHYSICAL DEVELOPMENT
- Perception

COGNITIVE DEVELOPMENT
* Progression of play
- Memory
- Connecting experiences
- Spatial awareness
- Following simple directions

LANGUAGE DEVELOPMENT
- Receptive language
- Connecting words with real-world knowledge
- Concept words
- Using language in play

Expand the Activity

Use the baby's photos and photos of the baby's family members to create a picture book. Read the book together by commenting on and talking about the photos. Create a book for each infant. Read the books to different infants, being sure to identify the photos—for example, say, "I know who this is. This is Jilly. And who is this? This is Jilly's daddy."

BUILD LANGUAGE SKILLS

Vocabulary

- Who
- Baby
- Names of different children in the group
- You
- Him
- Her
- He
- She
- Where
- Found
- Picture

Questions and Things to Say

"I am looking for a baby named Isabelle. Where is Isabelle?" When you find a photo of the baby, say, "Who is this baby? Is this Isabelle? Yes! This is Isabelle! This baby is you!"

Songs, Chants, and Fingerplays

Song: "Who's This Baby?" by Kimberly Bohannon
(Tune: "Frère Jacques")

Who's this baby?
Who's this baby?
This is you.
This is you.
This is Isabelle.
This is Isabelle.
This is you.
This is you.

Additional verses:
Insert the names of other children
into the song.

You Can Do It Too

MATERIALS

Suggested Books

- *Big Bird's Copycat Day* by Sharon Lerner
- *Can You? Waddle Like a Penguin*
  by Price Stern Sloan
- *Cookie See! Cookie Do!* by Anna Jane Hays
- *From Head to Toe* by Eric Carle
- *Monkey See, Monkey Do* by Helen Oxenbury

HOW TO DO IT

Sit with an infant on your lap or sit facing the infant if she is able to sit up by herself. Make a variety of movements with your hands, such as waving or wiggling your fingers; be sure to describe what you are doing. After each movement, ask the baby to do the same movement. If she is unable to, take her hands and gently make the movement for her. Read the suggested books, introduce the vocabulary words, and sing and chant with the infant.

Modifications for Toddlers and Twos

Ask the children to make movements for you to imitate. Or play music and ask them to move to the music by clapping hands or bouncing up and down—then you make the movements too.

Expand the Activity

Make simple movements with your mouth, such as opening and closing it, or make silly sounds with your mouth for the baby to imitate.

LEARNING OUTCOMES

SOCIAL–EMOTIONAL DEVELOPMENT
- Sense of self
- Personal identity
- Relationships with adults
- Self-regulation

PHYSICAL DEVELOPMENT
- Gross-motor skills
- Fine-motor skills
- Perception

COGNITIVE DEVELOPMENT
* Imitating others
* Following simple directions
- Cause and effect
- Memory
- Spatial awareness
- Connecting experiences

LANGUAGE DEVELOPMENT
- Receptive language
- Expressive language
- Connecting words with
  real-world knowledge
- Concept words
- Using language in play

BUILD LANGUAGE SKILLS

Vocabulary

- Move
- Touch

- Pat
- Clap

- Wiggle
- Tickle

- Wave bye-bye
- Wave hello

Questions and Things to Say

"Look how I am wiggling my fingers. Now you wiggle your fingers. Wiggle, wiggle, wiggle! Now I am patting my tummy. Can you pat your tummy too?"

Songs, Chants, and Fingerplays

Song: "Here We Go"
by Jean Barbre
(Tune: "Frère Jacques")

Watch me, watch me.
Watch me, watch me.
Here I go.
Here I go.
You can do it too.
You can do it too.
Here we go.
Here we go.

Fingerplay: "Pat-a-Cake" (traditional)
Fingerplay: "Hickory Dickory Dock" (traditional)

Ace in the Hole

MATERIALS

- Large-size stacking rings
- Pegboard and pegs
- Sorting cubes or buckets

Suggested Books

- *Colors, ABC, Numbers* by Roger Priddy
- *Roar! A Noisy Counting Book* by Pamela Duncan Edwards
- *White Rabbit's Color Book* by Alan Baker

HOW TO DO IT

Place the stacking rings or pegboard in front of the child. Model how to place the rings on the pole, pegs on the pegboard, or shapes into the sorting cubes or buckets. Talk about how there is a special space in the toy where the items are to be placed. At this age, the child's task is just to figure out how to place the rings on the pole, pegs in the pegboard, or items into the sorting cube. Identify the colors and shapes being used, but don't expect young children to place them in the correct spot. Read the suggested books, introduce the vocabulary words, and sing and chant with the children.

Modifications for Twos

Separate the items by colors or shapes. Focus on one color at a time; ask the child to identify another object that is the same color. In this version, simply introduce the concept of different colors. Don't expect the child to understand differences between colors.

Expand the Activity

Help the child sort items by color or shape. Count the pegs or rings while the child engages in the activity.

LEARNING OUTCOMES

SOCIAL-EMOTIONAL DEVELOPMENT
- Relationships with adults
- Self-regulation
- Sharing

PHYSICAL DEVELOPMENT
* Fine-motor skills

COGNITIVE DEVELOPMENT
* Memory
- Spatial awareness
- Number awareness
- Imitating others

LANGUAGE DEVELOPMENT
- Receptive language
- Expressive language
- Connecting words with real-world knowledge
- Concept words
- Using language in play

BUILD LANGUAGE SKILLS

Vocabulary

- Pegs
- Rings
- Board

- Hole
- Place
- Stack

- In
- Out
- Round

- Turn
- Twist
- Color names

Questions and Things to Say

"This is called a pegboard. There are holes in the board for each peg. Can you see the hole? Touch the peg and run your finger through the hole on the board. Watch while I put the peg in a hole on the board. Will you try with me? Look how we can stack one peg on top of another one."

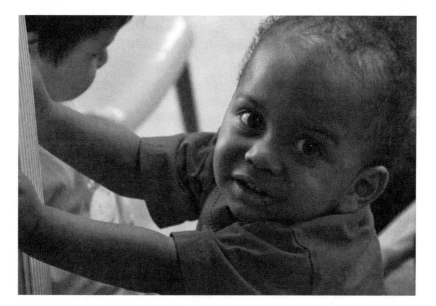

All About Apples

MATERIALS

- Three or four red apples
- Cutting board
- Vegetable peeler
- Sharp knife
- Plates, cups, or small bowls for serving

Suggested Books

- *The Apple Pie Tree* by Zoe Hall
- *Apples and Pumpkins* by Anne Rockwell
- *Baby Food* by Margaret Miller
- *First 100 Words* by Roger Priddy

HOW TO DO IT

Wash and dry the apples. Pass one around for the children to see and feel. Describe it. Cut the apple in half (along its equator) and show the children the inside. Talk about the seeds and the star design. Pull some of the seeds out and place them on a paper plate. Let the children examine the apple and the seeds. Serve unsweetened applesauce as a snack for the younger children. Read the suggested books, introduce the vocabulary words, and sing and chant with the children.

Modifications for Twos

After the children have looked at the apple, cut it in half. Pass around a magnifying class so the children can look at the seeds more closely. In a small group, ask them to share what they see, feel, and smell. Let them draw pictures of the apples, and write what they say on the back of their pictures. Cut clean, washed apples into slices and serve for snack.

LEARNING OUTCOMES

SOCIAL-EMOTIONAL DEVELOPMENT
- ★ Relationships with peers
- Personal identity
- Relationships with adults
- Sharing

PHYSICAL DEVELOPMENT
- Perception
- Fine-motor skills

COGNITIVE DEVELOPMENT
- Cause and effect
- Memory
- Spatial awareness
- Connecting experiences
- Number awareness
- Imitating others

LANGUAGE DEVELOPMENT
- ★ Using language in play
- Receptive language
- Expressive language
- Communicating needs
- Connecting words with real-world knowledge
- Concept words

Expand the Activity

Repeat the activity. Then peel the apples and cut them into small pieces. Place them in a heavy saucepan, add a few tables of water, and cook at medium heat until the apples are soft. Mash them or purée them in a blender until they're smooth. Add cinnamon to taste. Serve the homemade applesauce as a snack.

BUILD LANGUAGE SKILLS

Vocabulary

- Fruit
- Apple
- Peel
- Core
- Seeds
- Stem
- Star
- Red
- Waxy
- Inside
- Eat
- Crispy
- Juicy
- Cook
- Applesauce

Questions and Things to Say

"An apple is a fruit that's sweet and juicy. How many of you have tasted apples or applesauce? I'm going to pass the apple around for you to examine. What color is it? You're right, it's red. How does it feel? When I cut it in half, we can see the juice from the apple, the seeds, and a star design. I'm going to pass it around for you to see."

Songs, Chants, and Fingerplays

Song: "All About Apples" by Kimberly Bohannon
(Tune: "Frère Jacques")

Where is the apple?
Where is the apple?
Here it is.
Here it is.
Let's all smell the apple.
Let's all smell the apple.
Here it is.
Here it is.

Additional verses:
What does it taste like?
What does it taste like?
It tastes sweet.
It tastes sweet.
We all like apples.
We all like apples.
They taste sweet.
They taste sweet.
What does it look like?
What does it look like?
It is red.
It is red.
When we cut it open,
When we cut it open,
We see a star.
We see a star.

All the Bells and Whistles

MATERIALS

A variety of bells and whistles:
- Jingle bells
- School bells
- Cowbells
- Handbells
- Sports whistles
- Train whistles

Suggested Books

- *ABCDrive!* by Naomi Howland
- *I'm Your Bus* by Marilyn Singer
- *Whistle for Willie* by Ezra Jack Keats

HOW TO DO IT

Show the children the bells, and pass them around so the children can hold and feel them. Ring each bell and blow the whistles for the children to hear. Talk about the different sounds. Explain that the bell's clapper makes a sound when it strikes the bell's sides. Ring the bells softly first and then loudly. Explain how a whistle works and why it sounds different than the bells. Read the suggested books, introduce the vocabulary words, and sing and chant with the children.

Modifications for Twos

In a small group or at circle time, tap a wind chime and ask the children to listen to its sound. Explain that a wind chime's clapper makes sounds when it hits the hanging tubes. Place the wind chimes outdoors, and talk to the children about what they see and hear.

LEARNING OUTCOMES

SOCIAL-EMOTIONAL DEVELOPMENT
- Sense of self
- Relationships with adults
- Relationships with peers
- Self-regulation
- Sharing

PHYSICAL DEVELOPMENT
- Perception
- Fine-motor skills

COGNITIVE DEVELOPMENT
✱ Connecting experiences
- Cause and effect
- Memory
- Spatial awareness
- Number awareness
- Imitating others
- Following simple directions

LANGUAGE DEVELOPMENT
✱ Engaging in music, rhythm, and rhyme
- Receptive language
- Expressive language
- Connecting words with real world knowledge
- Concept words
- Using language in play

Expand the Activity

Make a handbell using a sturdy, disposable 6-inch plastic plate, four small jingle bells, and four short lengths of yarn. Punch four evenly spaced holes on the plate about an inch from the edge. Tie a jingle bell to a length of yarn and thread the yarn through the hole. Repeat with the other three bells and lengths of yarn. Shake to play.

BUILD LANGUAGE SKILLS

Vocabulary

- Bells
- Wind chimes
- Whistle
- Clapper
- Ring
- Wind
- Hang
- Noise
- Loud
- Soft
- Sound

Questions and Things to Say

"There are many different bells. Each of them makes a different sound when we ring it. Listen to the sound of this bell. Does the jingle bell sound the same or different from the handbell? What happens when we ring the two bells at the same time? Would you like to ring the bell?"

Songs, Chants, and Fingerplays

Song: "Ring the Bells" by Kimberly Bohannon
(Tune: "Row, Row, Row Your Boat")

Ring, ring, ring the bells.
Ring them soft and loud.
Ring them high and ring them low.
And listen to their sounds.

Song: "Jingle Bells" (traditional)

Beautiful Butterflies

MATERIALS

– Books about and photographs of butterflies

Suggested Books

– *Are You a Butterfly?* by Judy Allen and Tudor Humphries
– *Magnificent Monarchs* by Linda Glaser
– *The Very Hungry Caterpillar* by Eric Carle
– *Where Did the Butterfly Get Its Name?* by Melvin Berger and Gilda Berger

HOW TO DO IT

Show the children photographs of butterflies. Talk to them about the patterns and colors of the wings. Talk about what caterpillars look like and how butterflies develop from caterpillars and fly away. Read the suggested books, introduce the vocabulary words, and sing and chant with the children.

Modifications for Twos

Explain in more detail the life cycle of a butterfly, including how caterpillars feed on leaves, how the cocoon-like chrysalis functions, and how wings form. Look for butterflies outdoors or on a nature walk.

Expand the Activity

Create a butterfly garden by researching butterflies that are native to your area. Plant the plants and flowers that butterflies love to feed and lay their eggs on. Butterfly gardens can be any size that fits your program, from a window box to a part of the yard. This is a great way to connect children with real-world knowledge about nature and the environment.

LEARNING OUTCOMES

SOCIAL-EMOTIONAL DEVELOPMENT
* Caring for others
– Relationships with adults

PHYSICAL DEVELOPMENT
– Perception
– Fine-motor skills

COGNITIVE DEVELOPMENT
– Spatial awareness
– Connecting experiences
– Number awareness

LANGUAGE DEVELOPMENT
* Connecting words with real-world knowledge
– Receptive language
– Expressive language
– Concept words
– Engaging in print
– Using language in play

BUILD LANGUAGE SKILLS

Vocabulary

- Butterfly
- Insect
- Caterpillar
- Wings
- Eggs
- Leaves
- Fly
- Colors
- Patterns

Questions and Things to Say

"Butterflies are beautiful insects. They fly from flower to flower. There are different kinds of butterflies. They have different colors and patterns. What do you see when you look at this butterfly?"

Songs, Chants, and Fingerplays

Song: "Butterflies Are Flying" by Kimberly Bohannon
(Tune: "London Bridge Is Falling Down")

Butterflies are flying,
Flying, flying.
Butterflies are flying
In the sky.

Chant: "Butterfly Flight" by Kimberly Bohannon

Spread your wings out wide. *(Hold your arms out)*
Now, hold them by your side. *(Hug your arms to your body)*
It's time for butterflies to fly. *(Hold your arms out and fly around the room as you say the rest of the chant)*
It's time for butterflies to fly,
Soaring high up in the sky.
It's time for them to land
Softly on the ground. *(Come back to where you started and put your arms at your side)*

Big Ball, Little Ball

MATERIALS

- Soft or rubber balls of varying sizes:
  › Large balls (too big to swallow or choke on) for use with younger children
  › Small balls for use with older children who have more developed motor skills and dexterity

Suggested Books

- *Here Are My Hands* by Bill Martin Jr. and John Archambault
- *My Hands* by Aliki
- *Rosie's Walk* by Pat Hutchins
- *Where Is Baby's Beach Ball?* by Karen Katz

HOW TO DO IT

Sit on the floor with your feet touching or almost touching the child's feet. With two hands, roll the ball toward the child. Verbally describe what you are doing. Repeat the activity with the child rolling the ball toward you. Use different-size balls to change the game. Read the suggested books, introduce the vocabulary words, and sing and chant with the children.

Modifications for Twos

Repeat the activity with two to three children sitting in a circle with their feet touching at the center of the circle. Ask them to roll the ball to the child across from them. When they have mastered this task, add a second, smaller ball to the circle.

Expand the Activity

Other objects—small cars, trucks, or cubes—can be used for rolling.

LEARNING OUTCOMES

SOCIAL-EMOTIONAL DEVELOPMENT
- Sense of self
- Personal identity
- Relationships with adults
- Relationships with peers
- Self-regulation
- Sharing

PHYSICAL DEVELOPMENT
- Perception
- Gross-motor skills
- Fine-motor skills

COGNITIVE DEVELOPMENT
✱ Cause and effect
- Spatial awareness
- Connecting experiences
- Number awareness
- Imitating others
- Progression of play
- Following simple directions

LANGUAGE DEVELOPMENT
✱ Concept words
- Receptive language
- Expressive language
- Connecting words with real-world knowledge
- Using language in play

BUILD LANGUAGE SKILLS

Vocabulary

- Balls
- Large
- Small
- Size
- Roll
- Bump
- Fast
- Slow
- Spin
- Twirl
- Pass
- Back and forth
- Around
- Between
- Next
- Take turns
- Touch
- Feet
- Share

Questions and Things to Say

"We're going to roll the ball back and forth between us. Can you roll it back to me? Watch while the ball rolls and spins around. We are sharing the ball, when we pass it back and forth between us."

Songs, Chants, and Fingerplays

Song: "There's a Ball on the Ground"
by Jean Barbre
(Tune: "If You're Happy and You Know It")

There's a ball on the ground, on the ground.
There's a ball on the ground, on the ground.
Let's watch it roll our way
As it spins and twirls this way.
There's a ball on the ground, on the ground.
There's a ball on the ground, on the ground.
There's a ball on the ground, on the ground.
Let's pass it back and forth
As we share it all around.
There's a ball on the ground, on the ground.

29

Color We Will Go

MATERIALS

Suggested Books

- *Brown Bear, Brown Bear, What Do You See?* by Bill Martin Jr.
- *Colors, ABC, Numbers* by Roger Priddy
- *I'm Your Bus* by Marilyn Singer
- *White Rabbit's Color Book* by Alan Baker

HOW TO DO IT

Help the child learn the names of objects and colors. Walk with an infant in your arms or hold the hand of a toddler when you play this game. Name an object—say, a rubber duck—and then tell the child, "The rubber ducky is yellow." Point to the object and let the child touch and feel it. As you move from object to object, sing "A Color We Will Find," found on the next page. Repeat the song, identifying different colors and objects. Read the suggested books, introduce the vocabulary words, and sing and chant with the children.

Modifications for Twos

Ask the children to identify and collect objects that are the same color. Children can ask for your help.

Expand the Activity

Continue helping the children identify objects and begin sorting them by category, such as big, medium, or small, or by texture, such as smooth, rough, or slippery.

LEARNING OUTCOMES

SOCIAL-EMOTIONAL DEVELOPMENT
- Relationships with adults

PHYSICAL DEVELOPMENT
- Fine-motor skills

COGNITIVE DEVELOPMENT
- Memory
- Spatial awareness
- Connecting experiences
- Progression of play

LANGUAGE DEVELOPMENT
- ✱ Receptive language
- ✱ Expressive language
- Communicating needs
- Connecting words with real-world knowledge
- Concept words
- Engaging in music, rhythm, and rhyme
- Using language in play

BUILD LANGUAGE SKILLS

Vocabulary

– Colors
– Names of objects

Questions and Things to Say

"Where shall we look for something yellow? I see a yellow book and a yellow scarf. I think I see a toy green frog. Here it is. Look at the frog's big eyes and the brown spots on its back."

Songs, Chants, and Fingerplays

Song: "A Color We Will Find" by Jean Barbre
(Tune: "The Farmer in the Dell")

A yellow ducky we will find.
Ducky we will find.
Hi-Ho! The Derry O!
A yellow ducky we will find.

Additional verses:
A red ball.
A blue bucket.
A green frog.
An orange pumpkin.
A brown bear.

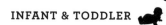

Do You Need a Hug?

MATERIALS

Suggested Books

- *How Do Dinosaurs Say I Love You?*
  by Jane Yolen and Mark Teague
- *How Do I Love You?* by Marion Dane Bauer
- *Hug* by Jez Alborough
- *Mommy Hugs* by Karen Katz

HOW TO DO IT

Hugs are a wonderful way for people to show they care about each other and to calm each other. Teach children about hugging by first giving them a hug. Ask them to wrap their arms around their own backs and give themselves a hug. Pass around a large doll or teddy bear for them to hug. Talk about how we squeeze when we hug, but not too tight! Tell them how hugs make us feel better when we're sad or when we've hurt our friends. Explain how hugs show love. Give lots of hugs and kisses to infants and toddlers to show them how much you care about them. Read the suggested books, introduce the vocabulary words, and sing and chant with the children.

LEARNING OUTCOMES

SOCIAL-EMOTIONAL DEVELOPMENT
* Self-regulation
- Sense of self
- Personal identity
- Relationships with adults
- Relationships with peers
- Empathy
- Caring for others

PHYSICAL DEVELOPMENT
- Perception
- Gross-motor skills

COGNITIVE DEVELOPMENT
- Spatial awareness
- Connecting experiences
- Imitating others

LANGUAGE DEVELOPMENT
* Communicating needs
- Connecting words with real-world knowledge
- Concept words
- Engaging in print

Modifications for Twos

Encourage children to express their love and affection for others by hugging their friends. Explain to toddlers and two-year-olds that they can give hugs anytime, but it's polite to first ask their friends, "Do you need a hug?"

Expand the Activity

Explain that there are other ways of showing people we care about them. Teach toddlers and two-year-olds how to give "high fives," "thumbs up," and blow kisses. Read the suggested books to the children.

BUILD LANGUAGE SKILLS

Vocabulary

- Hugs
- Arms
- Around
- Friends
- Comfort
- Caring
- Forgiveness
- Sorry
- Polite
- Happy
- Love

Questions and Things to Say

"Hugs make us feel better when we're sad. Can I give you a hug? When our friends are sad, we can ask them if they want hugs. Asking first is a polite thing to do to show we care."

Songs, Chants, and Fingerplays

Song: "Give a Big Hug" by Kimberly Bohannon
(Tune: "Frère Jacques")

Give a big hug.
Give a big hug.
Show you care.
Show you care.
You are very special.
You are very special.
Here's a hug.
Here's a hug.

Give a high five.
Give a high five.
Show you care.
Show you care.
You are very special.
You are very special.
Let's high five.
Let's high five.

Blow a big kiss.
Blow a big kiss.
Show you care.
Show you care.
You are very special.
You are very special.
Blow a kiss.
Blow a kiss.

Eye Spy

MATERIALS

- Small, clear plastic containers with lids
- Tray
- Labels
- Magnifying glass
- An assortment of items to explore (such as small rocks, seashells, beans, buttons, feathers, and corks)

Suggested Books

- *Black and White Rabbit's ABC* by Alan Baker
- *First 100 Words* by Roger Priddy
- *Richard Scarry's Best First Book Ever!* by Richard Scarry

HOW TO DO IT

Introduce one item at a time to the children. Place each one on a tray to provide a neutral background, and let the children examine them. Describe what they are seeing and feeling. Sort items, place each group in a clear plastic container, and secure the lid tightly. Place a label on each container identifying its contents. Let the children pick up the containers, shake them, and look at the items by rotating the containers. Talk to them about what they're seeing and hearing. Read the suggested books and introduce the vocabulary words to the children.

Modifications for Twos

Let the children choose additional items to place in new containers. You may find things on outdoor walks, such as nontoxic leaves or pieces of tree bark on the ground. Let the children look at the items with a magnifying glass. Talk to them about what they see and feel.

LEARNING OUTCOMES

SOCIAL-EMOTIONAL DEVELOPMENT
- Sense of self
- Personal identity
- Relationships with adults
- Relationships with peers
- Sharing

PHYSICAL DEVELOPMENT
- Perception
- Fine-motor skills

COGNITIVE DEVELOPMENT
- ✱ Progression of play
- Cause and effect
- Memory
- Spatial awareness
- Number awareness

LANGUAGE DEVELOPMENT
- ✱ Expressive language
- Receptive language
- Connecting words with real-world knowledge
- Concept words
- Engaging in print

Expand the Activity

Put two or three items together on a tray and let the children begin to sort, categorize, and name them before you put them in the plastic containers. Talk with the children about the different sounds the items make when you shake the containers. Compare and contrast them with other items in the classroom.

BUILD LANGUAGE SKILLS

Vocabulary

- Clear container
- Look
- Examine
- Lid
- Label
- Tray

- Rocks
- Seashells
- Beans
- Buttons
- Feathers
- Corks

- Size
- Large
- Small
- Round
- Smooth
- Rough

- Soft
- Top
- Bottom

Questions and Things to Say

"We're going to look at different items today. I've placed these colorful feathers on the tray for you to examine. Touch them and see what they feel like. Do they feel soft? Does it tickle when I place one next to your face? The feathers are different colors. Here's a red one and a green one. Let's place them in the container and look at them again. What sound do you hear when you shake the container?"

Feeling Free

MATERIALS

– Hand mirror
– Books showing children expressing emotions

Suggested Books

– *The Kissing Hand* by Audrey Penn
– *Lots of Feelings* by Shelley Rotner
– *On Monday When It Rained* by Cherryl Kachenmeister

HOW TO DO IT

Children are learning to identify their feelings and the feelings of others. Children can learn a lot about feelings by watching and observing others. In small-group time or with individual children, read a book that describes feelings and emotions, such as *Lots of Feelings*. Point to the feeling words and show the corresponding expression. Invite the children to imitate the expression. Use the hand mirror to let them see their facial expressions. Read the suggested books, introduce the vocabulary words, and sing and chant with the children.

Modifications for Twos

Expand children's feelings vocabulary and read stories such as *On Monday When It Rained* to help them understand feelings.

Expand the Activity

Discuss the story with the children and ask them draw faces showing

LEARNING OUTCOMES

SOCIAL–EMOTIONAL DEVELOPMENT
* Empathy
* Caring for others
– Sense of self
– Personal identity
– Relationships with adults
– Relationships with peers
– Self-regulation

PHYSICAL DEVELOPMENT
– Perception

COGNITIVE DEVELOPMENT
– Connecting experiences
– Imitating others

LANGUAGE DEVELOPMENT
– Receptive language
– Expressive language
– Communicating needs
– Connecting words with real-world knowledge
– Concept words
– Engaging in print

different feelings. To build empathy and caring, ask them how they could help a child who is feeling sad or afraid.

BUILD LANGUAGE SKILLS

Vocabulary

- Happy
- Excited
- Sad
- Afraid
- Scared
- Surprised
- Angry

Questions and Things to Say

"There are many different feelings. As we look at our book, we can see the children's faces. Here's a child who is happy. Let's make a happy face. I see you smiling. Look at yourself in the mirror. How does it look if we're feeling sad?"

Songs, Chants, and Fingerplays

Song: "If You're Happy and You Know It" (traditional)
Additional verses by Jean Barbre:

If you're sad and you know it, say "Boo hoo."
If you're sad and you know it, say "Boo hoo."
If you're sad and you know it, then your face will surely show it,
If you're sad and you know it, say "Boo hoo."

If you're angry and you know it, make a frown.
If you're angry and you know it, make a frown.
If you're angry and you know it, then your face will surely show it,
If you're angry and you know it, make a frown.

If you're tired and you know it, rub your eyes.
If you're tired and you know it, rub your eyes.
If you're tired and you know it, then your face will surely show it,
If you're tired and you know it, rub your eyes.

Flower Power

MATERIALS

– Masking tape
– Scissors
– Items found on a nature walk

Suggested Books

– *Bugs! Bugs! Bugs!* by Bob Barner
– *Counting in the Garden* by Kim Parker
– *The Surprise Garden* by Zoe Hall

HOW TO DO IT

Cut a piece of masking tape to fit loosely around a toddler's wrist. Tape the ends together, sticky side out. If you are working with infants, you may want to put tape on your own wrist, sticky side out, for this activity. Go for a walk outdoors, and look for flowers growing in the garden or walkway. Allow children to pick leaves and flower petals off the ground and place them on the tape. Have them smell the flower petals and leaves on their wrists. Ask them what they liked about the nature walk.

LEARNING OUTCOMES

SOCIAL-EMOTIONAL DEVELOPMENT
– Sense of self
– Relationships with adults
– Relationships with peers
– Self-regulation
– Empathy
– Caring for others
– Sharing

PHYSICAL DEVELOPMENT
– Perception
– Fine-motor skills

COGNITIVE DEVELOPMENT
✱ Connecting experiences
✱ Following simple directions
– Cause and effect
– Memory
– Spatial awareness
– Imitating others

LANGUAGE DEVELOPMENT
– Receptive language
– Expressive language
– Connecting words with real-world knowledge
– Concept words
– Using language in play

Be sure they don't put any of the items in their mouths! Read the suggested books, introduce the vocabulary words, and sing and chant with the children.

Modifications for Twos

Bring three or four different flowers to class for the children to examine. Ask them to smell a flower and pass it on to the next child. Encourage them to say, "Would you like to smell the flower?" Place the items you collect on the nature walk in a vase and place the vase on the snack table as a centerpiece.

Expand the Activity

Take a magnifying glass on the nature walk to look closely at the flower petals and leaves, and talk about what the children see. Share the importance of caring for nature and the environment. Watch out for bees!

BUILD LANGUAGE SKILLS

Vocabulary

- Masking tape
- Wrist
- Nature walk
- Sticky
- Place
- Smell
- Flower petal
- Leaves
- Like (in phrases such as *smells like*)

Questions and Things to Say

"We're going on a nature walk to look at flowers and leaves. The tape on your wrist is like a bracelet. We're going to stick the flower petals and leaves we find on the ground on it. Here's a flower petal. What does is smell like? How does the leaf feel?"

Songs, Chants, and Fingerplays

Song: "Bring Back a Flower for Me"
by Kimberly Bohannon
(Tune: "My Bonnie Lies over the Ocean")

The flowers grow in the garden.
They start as tiny seeds.
The petals bloom, bright and open
On top of the stem and leaves.
Flowers, flowers,
Blooming so fresh and free.
Flowers, flowers,
Bring back a flower for me.

Chant: "We're Going on a Nature Walk"
by Kimberly Bohannon

We're going on a nature walk.
We're going on a nature walk.
We're going to find some flowers.
We're going to find some flowers.
Where are they?
Where are they?
There they are.

Additional verses:
You can substitute leaves for flowers or any other items that you find outdoors.

34

Friends on the Farm

MATERIALS

- Picture and storybooks with farm animals
- Toy farm sets
- Toy farm animals

Suggested Books

- *Click, Clack, Quackity-Quack: An Alphabetical Adventure* by Doreen Cronin
- *Farm Animals* by Phoebe Dunn
- *Mrs. Wishy-Washy's Farm* by Joy Cowley
- *My Big Animal Book* by Roger Priddy
- *Open the Barn Door. . .* by Christopher Santoro

HOW TO DO IT

Collect books, toy farm sets, and farm animals. Sit on the floor with the children, and read one of the suggested books. Show them a picture of a farm and describe the farm setting, including the barn and farm animals. Encourage the children to play with the farm sets, and show and name the farm animals. Let the children imitate the sounds of the animals and play with the farm set together. Introduce the vocabulary words and sing and chant with the children.

Modifications for Twos

Repeat the activity above, and describe the farm in more detail. For example, talk about what the farmer does. Describe the tools and machines used on the farm, what the animals eat, and what food we get from the animals on the farms.

Expand the Activity

Plant a small garden with the children and document its growth visually on a poster, beginning with a photograph of the seeds being planted. Take photographs of the children helping in the garden, and post them for parents and children to see.

LEARNING OUTCOMES

SOCIAL-EMOTIONAL DEVELOPMENT
- Relationships with adults
- Relationships with peers
- Empathy
- Caring for others
- Sharing

PHYSICAL DEVELOPMENT
- Fine-motor skills

COGNITIVE DEVELOPMENT
✳ Imitating others
- Memory
- Spatial awareness
- Connecting experiences
- Number awareness
- Progression of play

LANGUAGE DEVELOPMENT
✳ Engaging in print
- Receptive language
- Expressive language
- Using language in play

BUILD LANGUAGE SKILLS

Vocabulary

- Farm
- Farm animals
- Farmer
- Cow
- Pig
- Horse
- Duck
- Chickens
- Rabbits
- Barn
- Tractor
- Hay
- Feed

Questions and Things to Say

"Many different animals are on farms. Here is a picture of a cow, a pig, and a horse. Can you point to the cow? The cow says *moo*. Say *moo* with me. That's great. The pig says *oink oink*. Say that with me, *oink oink*. The farmer is the person who takes care of all the animals on the farm."

Songs, Chants, Fingerplays

Song: "Old MacDonald Had a Farm" (traditional)

35

Garden Footprints

MATERIALS

- Green, yellow, pink, red, and black tempera paint
- Bucket of water
- A long piece of butcher paper
- Small containers or pie pans
- Black marker
- Sponge brushes
- Water
- Paper towels

Suggested Books

- *Counting in the Garden* by Kim Parker
- *Ten Little Fingers* by Annie Kubler
- *This Little Piggy* by Annie Kubler

HOW TO DO IT

Tape the butcher paper to the floor. Place the green paint in a small container or pie pan, and sponge green paint on the bottom 2 or 3 inches of the paper. This will be the grass for the flowers. Place the yellow, pink, and red paint in separate containers. Remove the children's shoes, and have them pick a color. Helping the children one at a time, paint the bottoms of their feet and ask them to step on the paper atop the green paint. They may need some assistance stepping off the paper. Wash the paint off their feet and dry them. Once the footprints have dried, draw the stems on the flowers, using the sponge brush and the black paint. Label the flowers with the children's names. Hang the Garden Footprints in the classroom. Read the suggested books, introduce the vocabulary words, and sing and chant with the children.

Modifications for Twos

Have children help paint the grass on the bottom of the paper.

LEARNING OUTCOMES

SOCIAL-EMOTIONAL DEVELOPMENT
- ✱ Personal identity
- Sense of self
- Relationships with adults
- Relationships with peers
- Self-regulation
- Sharing

PHYSICAL DEVELOPMENT
- Perception
- Gross-motor skills

COGNITIVE DEVELOPMENT
- ✱ Following simple directions
- Cause and effect
- Memory
- Spatial awareness
- Connecting experiences
- Imitating others

LANGUAGE DEVELOPMENT
- Receptive language
- Expressive language
- Connecting words with real-world knowledge
- Concept words
- Engaging in print

Expand the Activity

Invite children to create their own footprint pages on large pieces of construction paper. They can also paint a sun or clouds on the mural.

BUILD LANGUAGE SKILLS

Vocabulary

- Paint
- Sponge
- Brush
- Paper
- Bucket
- Grass
- Flowers
- Feet
- Footprint
- Step
- Place
- Wet
- Dry
- Wash

Questions and Things to Say

"You chose yellow. We're going to paint your feet with yellow paint. How does the paint feel on your feet? Place your feet on the paper. Look at your footprints on the paper. Step in the bucket, so I can wash the paint off. Now it's Tony's turn."

Songs, Chants, and Fingerplays

Song: "Did You Ever See a Flower?"
by Kimberly Bohannon
(Tune: "Did You Ever See a Lassie?")

Did you ever see a flower,
A flower, a flower?
Did you ever see a flower
With petals and leaves?
Growing this way and that way
And this way and that way.
Did you ever see a flower with petals
and leaves?

Additional verses:
Other objects, such as a rainbow, ladybug, spider, or butterfly.

Song: "Bring Back a Flower for Me"
by Kimberly Bohannon
(Tune: "My Bonnie Lies over the Ocean")

The flowers grow in the garden.
They start as tiny seeds.
The petals bloom bright and open
On top of the stem and leaves.
Flowers, flowers,
Blooming so fresh and free.
Flowers, flowers,
Bring back a flower for me.

Hats Off to You

MATERIALS

- A variety of adult-size hats with firm brims (which are easy for younger children to put on and take off)
- A mirror

Suggested Books

- *Blue Hat, Green Hat* by Sandra Boynton
- *Hats* by Debbie Bailey
- *Hats, Hats, Hats* by Ann Morris
- *Whose Hat Is This? A Look at Hats Workers Wear— Hard, Tall, and Shiny* by Sharon Katz Cooper

HOW TO DO IT

Children delight in putting hats on and off themselves, adults, and peers. Select a hat, such as one worn by a construction worker. Describe the color of the hat, and show the children how to place the hats on their heads. Show them how they look in the mirror. Place one of the other hats on your own head and describe it to another child. Young children may prefer to place the hat on and off your head at first. Read the suggested books, introduce the vocabulary words, and sing and chant with the children.

Modifications for Twos

As children engage in more dramatic play, they enjoy using hats imaginatively. Add other items to the dramatic play area that corresponds to the hats, such as a tool belt, toy tools, and boots for a construction worker.

Expand the Activity

Use a different theme for the dramatic play area, such as a construction site, bakery, or camping area. Include items for that theme, including puppets or stuffed animals with hats on their heads.

LEARNING OUTCOMES

SOCIAL-EMOTIONAL DEVELOPMENT
- ★ Sense of self
- ★ Sharing
- Personal identity
- Relationships with adults
- Relationships with peers

PHYSICAL DEVELOPMENT
- Gross-motor skills

COGNITIVE DEVELOPMENT
- Cause and effect
- Memory
- Spatial awareness
- Connecting experiences
- Imitating others
- Progression of play
- Following simple directions

LANGUAGE DEVELOPMENT
- Receptive language
- Expressive language
- Connecting words with real-world knowledge
- Concept words
- Using language in play

BUILD LANGUAGE SKILLS

Vocabulary

- On
- Off
- Up
- Down
- Front
- Back
- Mine
- Yours
- Share
- Place
- Wear
- Top
- Brim
- Plastic
- Straw

Questions and Things to Say

"Watch while I put the yellow hat on my head. Put the hat on my head. Can you take it off? Look at yourself in the mirror. This hat is worn by a construction worker. Now, let's ask Miguel if he wants to wear the hat."

Songs, Chants, and Fingerplays

Song: "There's a Hat on My Head"
by Kimberly Bohannon
(Tune: "The Farmer in the Dell")

There's a hat on my head.
There's a hat on my head.
It's called a *hard hat*.
There's a hard hat on my head.

There's a hat on my head.
There's a hat on my head.
It's called a *chef's hat*.
There's a chef's hat on my head.

There's a hat on my head.
There's a hat on my head.
It's called a *cowboy hat*.
There's a cowboy hat on my head.

There's a hat on my head.
There's a hat on my head.
It's called a *top hat*.
There's a top hat on my head.

There's a hat on my head.
There's a hat on my head.
It's called a *straw hat*.
There's a straw hat on my head.

Chant: "Hats All Around"
by Kimberly Bohannon
(Start the chant by having the child pick a hat and put it on.)

Hats, hats, all around.
Some are tall and others round.
Raise your hat up. Now, put it down.
Find a new hat. There're hats all around.
Hats, hats, all around.

Hello and Good-bye Kisses

MATERIALS

Suggested Books

- *Hello! Good-bye!* by Aliki
- *How Do I Love You?* by Marion Dane Bauer
- *The Kissing Hand* by Audrey Penn
- *When I Miss You* by Cornelia Maude Spelman

HOW TO DO IT

Saying "hello" and "good-bye" is an important part of building relationships with adults and peers. Adults can show babies how to wave hello and good-bye. Blowing kisses is another way of showing others that we care about them. Model and encourage these social exchanges when children arrive at your program in the morning and leave at the end of the day. Read the suggested books, introduce the vocabulary words, and sing and chant with the children.

Modifications for Twos

As children arrive, meet and greet each of them and encourage them to wave hello to the children who are already there. At the end of the day, ask the children to wave good-bye and blow kisses when others leave for the day.

Expand the Activity

Talk about how it feels when children miss their parents. Teach them new feeling words to use. Ask them to draw a picture to give to their parents. Read the suggested books to the children.

LEARNING OUTCOMES

SOCIAL-EMOTIONAL DEVELOPMENT
- ✱ Relationships with peers
- Sense of self
- Personal identity
- Relationships with adults
- Empathy
- Caring for others

PHYSICAL DEVELOPMENT
- Fine-motor skills

COGNITIVE DEVELOPMENT
- Memory
- Connecting experiences
- Imitating others

LANGUAGE DEVELOPMENT
- ✱ Communication of needs
- Receptive language
- Expressive language
- Connecting words with real-world knowledge
- Concept words
- Engaging in print

BUILD LANGUAGE SKILLS

Vocabulary

– Hello	– Blow	– Friends	– Scared
– Good-bye	– Kisses	– Miss	– Cheerful
– Bye	– Hands	– Happy	– Joyful
– Wave	– Greet	– Sad	– Excited

Questions and Things to Say

"Let's blow a kiss as we say good-bye to Mommy. Say good-bye and wave. She'll be back later today. Here's our friend Tommy—let's wave hello to him. We're happy he's here today to play with us."

Songs, Chants, and Fingerplays

Song: "Hello and Good-bye"
by Kimberly Bohannon
(Tune: "Frère Jacques")

Wave hello,
Wave hello
To a friend,
To a friend.
We're going to have a good day.
We're going to have a good day.
Wave hello
To your friend.

Blow a kiss,
Blow a kiss
To a friend,
To a friend.
We'll see you tomorrow.
We'll see you tomorrow.
Blow a kiss
To your friend.

Wave good-bye,
Wave good-bye
To a friend,
To a friend.
We'll see you tomorrow.
We'll see you tomorrow.
Wave good-bye
To your friend.

38

Let's Play Together

MATERIALS

Suggested Books

- *Eyes, Nose, Fingers, and Toes: A First Book All About You* by Judy Hindley
- *Mommy's Little Star* by Janet Bingham
- *My Hands* by Aliki
- *This Little Piggy* by Annie Kubler
- *The Very Busy Spider: A Lift-the-Flap Book* by Eric Carle

HOW TO DO IT

Teach the children fingerplays, such as the ones suggested on the next page or one of your own favorites. Seat the child in your lap while you show her how to do the fingerplays. Although babies can't do the activity alone, they will enjoy hearing the words and watching you. As they get older and repeat the fingerplay, they will begin to imitate and join you. Read the suggested books, introduce the vocabulary words, and sing "Friends at School" (found on the next page) with the children.

Modifications for Twos

With practice, children become more skilled at the fingerplays and better at saying or singing the words. Once they engage in parallel play, they enjoy joining you and their peers in these activities.

Expand the Activity

Read *The Very Busy Spider: A Lift-the-Flap Book* or *Mommy's Little Star* and encourage the children to create pictures of stars or spiders, using crayons, markers, tissue paper, and glue.

LEARNING OUTCOMES

SOCIAL-EMOTIONAL DEVELOPMENT
✴ Relationships with adults
- Sense of self
- Personal identity
- Relationships with peers
- Self-regulation

PHYSICAL DEVELOPMENT
- Fine-motor skills

COGNITIVE DEVELOPMENT
✴ Progression of play
- Memory
- Connecting experiences
- Imitating others
- Following simple directions

LANGUAGE DEVELOPMENT
- Receptive language
- Expressive language
- Connecting words with real-world knowledge
- Concept words
- Engaging in print
- Engaging in music, rhythm, and rhyme
- Using language in play

BUILD LANGUAGE SKILLS

Vocabulary

- Fingers
- Toes
- Hands
- Play
- Twinkle

- Star
- Thumb
- Open
- Shut
- Spider

- Crawl
- Down
- Up

Questions and Things to Say

"Come and sit with me while we sing the song "Twinkle, Twinkle, Little Star." Watch how I move my fingers this way. Let's do it together. I'll help you. There you go. You did it! Shall we sing it again?"

Songs, Chants, and Fingerplays

Song: "Friends at School" by Jean Barbre (Tune: "Frère Jacques")

Play together, play together.
Let's have fun, let's have fun.
We have fun together.
We have fun together.
Friends at school, friends at school.

Fingerplay: "Twinkle, Twinkle, Little Star" (traditional)
Fingerplay: "Where Is Thumbkin?" (traditional)
Fingerplay: "Open, Shut Them" (traditional)
Fingerplay: "Itsy, Bitsy Spider" (traditional)
Fingerplay: "This Little Piggy" (traditional)

39

Move It, Shake It

MATERIALS

- Musical instruments that are easy for young children to grip and use (such as wrist and ankle bells, egg shakers, maracas, cymbals, tambourines, and rhythm sticks)
- Music with a variety of different rhythms (such as Greg and Steve's *Shake, Rattle, and Rock* and *We All Live Together*, volume 5)

Suggested Books

- *Barnyard Dance!* by Sandra Boynton
- *Giraffes Can't Dance* by Giles Andreae
- *Mouse's First Day of School* by Lauren Thompson
- *Too Loud Lily* by Sofie Laguna

HOW TO DO IT

Each week, introduce the children to a new instrument. Describe it and encourage the children to touch it and hear it played. Model how to use the instrument while you sing a song or play music. Show young infants or toddlers how to shake the bells or maracas. Let them use the instruments while you're singing or playing. Leave the instruments where children can easily reach them to use for play. Read the suggested books, introduce the vocabulary words, and sing and chant with the children.

Modifications for Twos

With a small group of children, sing and clap to a familiar song, such as "Row, Row, Row, Your Boat." Talk to the children about rhythm in music. Demonstrate how to use an instrument while you sing a familiar song. Introduce another instrument to the group and repeat the activity. Encourage the children to pass the instruments around so they learn to share and take turns.

LEARNING OUTCOMES

SOCIAL-EMOTIONAL DEVELOPMENT
- Sense of self
- Relationships with adults
- Relationships with peers
- Self-regulation
- Sharing

PHYSICAL DEVELOPMENT
- Perception
- Fine-motor skills

COGNITIVE DEVELOPMENT
★ Cause and effect
- Memory
- Spatial awareness
- Connecting experiences
- Number awareness
- Imitating others
- Progression of play
- Following simple directions

LANGUAGE DEVELOPMENT
★ Engaging in music, rhythm, and rhyme
- Receptive language
- Expressive language
- Connecting words with real-world knowledge
- Concept words

Expand the Activity

Have each child pick an instrument and form a circle. Play a familiar song, and let the children practice their instruments. Ask them to identify the instruments they are using. Ask them to march around the room, listening and playing to the music. When the song is over, invite the children to exchange their instrument for another and play the song again.

BUILD LANGUAGE SKILLS

Vocabulary

- Instruments
- Bells
- Egg shakers
- Maracas
- Cymbals
- Tambourines
- Rhythm sticks
- Rhythm
- Beat
- Sound
- Noise
- Pass
- Share
- Hear
- Handle
- Shiny
- Touch
- Music
- Songs

Questions and Things to Say

"These are bells. I'm going to give each of you a handbell. Now shake your hand and hear the sound the bell makes. The bells are shiny and have handles. Here's a maraca—it makes a sound too. Listen to the sound it makes. How does it sound different from the bells?"

Songs, Chants, and Fingerplays

Song: "Play Your Instrument" by Jean Barbre
(Tune: "Row, Row, Row Your Boat")

Make, make, make a sound,
Make it high or low.
Play it fast, play it slow,
Anywhere we go!

Tap, tap, tap your drum,
Hit it high or low.
Tap your drum,
Tap your drum,
Hear its rum-tum-tum.

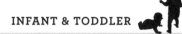

40

Movin' and Groovin' with My Friends

MATERIALS

– Music with a variety of rhythms
  (such as Greg and Steve's *Kids in Motion*,
  Jumpin' and Jammin' or *Shake, Rattle and Rock*)
– Stuffed animals
– Dolls

Suggested Books

– *Barnyard Dance!* by Sandra Boynton
– *Dancing Feet!* by Lindsey Craig
– *Giraffes Can't Dance* by Giles Andreae
– *Rosie's Walk* by Pat Hutchins

HOW TO DO IT

Children love to dance and move to music. Demonstrate how we sometimes dance alone and other
times with a friend. Invite a child to dance with
you, then ask the children to pick a friend or a
stuffed animal or doll to dance with. Introduce
concept words, like *go, stop, begin, end, around,
under, over, right, left, swing, twist, turn, high,* and
low while you play the music. Be sure there's plenty of room for children to move freely.
You can hold babies while you dance to the music. Read the suggested books, introduce the
vocabulary words, and sing and chant with the children.

Modifications for Twos

Give the children scarves and hats to wear while they move and grove to the music. Video-
tape them dancing and play the recording back for them.

LEARNING OUTCOMES

SOCIAL-EMOTIONAL DEVELOPMENT
– Sense of self
– Relationships with adults
– Relationships with peers
– Sharing

PHYSICAL DEVELOPMENT
– Perception
– Gross-motor skills
– Fine-motor skills

COGNITIVE DEVELOPMENT
– Spatial awareness
– Connecting experiences
– Imitating others
– Progression of play

LANGUAGE DEVELOPMENT
✷ Concept words
✷ Engaging in music, rhythm,
  and rhyme
– Receptive language
– Expressive language
– Connecting words with
  real-world knowledge

Expand the Activity

Repeat the activity outdoors on the grass. If possible, have the children dance in their bare feet.

BUILD LANGUAGE SKILLS

Vocabulary

– Music	– Begin	– Right	– High
– Dance	– End	– Left	– Low
– Friends	– Around	– Swing	
– Go	– Under	– Twist	
– Stop	– Over	– Turn	

Questions and Things to Say

"We're going to dance with our friends today. Who wants to dance with me? Watch as I twirl Frankie under my arm. Now we're going to twist in a circle. Pick a friend, a stuffed animal, or a doll, and I'll play the music again."

Songs, Chants, and Fingerplays

Song: "Dancing Shoes"
by Kimberly Bohannon
(Tune: "Mary Had a Little Lamb")

Our class has their dancing shoes,
Dancing shoes, dancing shoes.
Our class has their dancing shoes,
Dancing all day long.

Additional verses:
Replace "our class" with a child's name.

Chant: "Twist and Twirl" by Kimberly Bohannon

Get your body movin',
Get your body groovin',
And twist and twirl
And twist and twirl.

Twist your body fast,
Twist your body slow,
And twist and twirl
And twist and twirl.

Twirl to the left,
Twirl to the right,
And twist and twirl
And twist and twirl.

Get your body movin',
Get your body groovin',
And twist and twirl
And twist and twirl.

My Family

MATERIALS

– Pictures of each child's family
– Glue
– Poster boards

Suggested Books

– *Bear's Busy Family* by Stella Blackstone
– *How Do I Love You?* by Marion Dane Bauer
– *Mama Zooms* by Jane Cowen-Fletcher
– *You and Me Together: Moms, Dads, and Kids Around the World* by Barbara Kerley

HOW TO DO IT

Ask families to bring in family photographs and have them label the people and activities in them. Help the children identify the people in the photographs by name. Place each child's family photo on a separate poster board. Post them at eye level, where the child can see them. Talk about how families are special and unique. Read the suggested books, introduce the vocabulary words, and sing and chant with the children.

Modifications for Twos

Let the children take turns talking about their family at circle time. Have them draw pictures of their family. Write what they say on the back of the paper.

Expand the Activity

Ask each child's family to send something representing their cultural background to class. Let the children take turns sharing these things. If items can be left, group them in a safe area of the classroom for further viewing.

LEARNING OUTCOMES

SOCIAL–EMOTIONAL DEVELOPMENT
✽ Relationships with adults
– Sense of self
– Personal identity
– Relationships with peers
– Empathy
– Caring for others
– Sharing

PHYSICAL DEVELOPMENT
– Perception

COGNITIVE DEVELOPMENT
– Memory
– Connecting experiences

LANGUAGE DEVELOPMENT
✽ Receptive language
– Expressive language
– Communicating needs
– Connecting words with real-world knowledge
– Concept words

BUILD LANGUAGE SKILLS

Vocabulary

- Family
- Pictures
- Mom
- Dad
- Grandma

- Grandpa
- Sister
- Brother
- Aunt
- Uncle

- Home
- Love
- Pets

Questions and Things to Say

"Every family is different and special. Our families are the people that love us. Here are pictures of your family. Who is this? Is that your grandmother? You look like you're having fun playing with your dog. Is this when your family went to the park? What did you do at the park?"

Songs, Chants, and Fingerplays

Chant: "You Have a Family" by Kimberly Bohannon

You have a family.
Yes, you do.
You have a family.
They love you.

You have a family.
Yes, you do.
Who's in your family?
(Ask a child to point to someone in the picture or to say a name.)
She loves you. *(Replace* she *with the person the child names or points to.)*

42

My Five Little Senses

MATERIALS

- A variety of sensory objects (including real objects, such as fruits, flowers, leaves, and wood)
- Cotton balls
- Baking extracts to drop on cotton balls (such as vanilla, almond, or orange)

Suggested Books

- *Baby Touch and Feel Animals* by DK Publishing
- *Don't Touch, It's Hot* by David Algrim
- *My Five Senses* by Aliki
- *My Five Senses* by Margaret Miller

HOW TO DO IT

Collect the sensory items and introduce the children to the five senses. Have children touch their ears, eyes, noses, tongues, and fingertips. Pass the sensory items around one at a time for the children to touch, feel, and smell. Describe the objects and scents, and help the children make connections with their senses. Explain how we use our sense of smell and taste when we eat. Tell them that things feel different when we touch them—for example, the teddy bear is soft and the wood feels rough. Connect the senses to other activities, such as All the Bells and Whistles (activity 26), Orange Peel (activity 82), or March to the Drum (activity 80). Read the suggested books, introduce the vocabulary words, and sing and chant with the children.

Modifications for Twos

Invite the children to play a sensory game. One at a time, ask them either to close their eyes or cover their eyes with their hands. Place an object, such as a strawberry or a slice of orange, under their noses, and see if they can guess what it is. Continue this game with other objects that require using all five senses. Explain how we have different likes and dislikes in what we taste and smell.

LEARNING OUTCOMES

SOCIAL-EMOTIONAL DEVELOPMENT
- ✱ Empathy
- – Sense of self
- – Relationships with adults
- – Relationships with peers
- – Sharing

PHYSICAL DEVELOPMENT
- – Perception
- – Fine-motor skills

COGNITIVE DEVELOPMENT
- – Memory
- – Spatial awareness
- – Connecting experiences
- – Imitating others

LANGUAGE DEVELOPMENT
- ✱ Using language in play
- – Receptive language
- – Expressive language
- – Connecting words with real-world knowledge
- – Concept words

Expand the Activity

Take the children on a nature walk. Stop and examine different items, and have the children explore them with their senses. Place the objects in a basket or on a tray where the children can easily examine them.

BUILD LANGUAGE SKILLS

Vocabulary

- Five senses
- Close
- Cover
- Ears
- Eyes
- Nose
- Tongue
- Fingers

Questions and Things to Say

"We explore the world through our five senses. Our senses tell us what we hear, see, smell, taste, and feel. Touch your ears and tell me what you hear when I play the maracas. How do they sound different from the jingle bell? With our fingers we feel things. How does the teddy bear feel? Is he soft? Here's a rubber ball. How does the teddy bear feel differently than the rubber ball?"

Songs, Chants, and Fingerplays

Song: "Dancing Shoes" by Kimberly Bohannon
(Tune: "Mary Had a Little Lamb")

Flowers, flowers smell so sweet,
Smell so sweet,
Smell so sweet.
Flowers, flowers smell so sweet,
Let's put them in a vase.

Teddy, Teddy feels so soft,
Feels so soft,
Feels so soft.
Teddy, Teddy feels so soft,
Let's give him a big hug.

My Little Cubby

MATERIALS

– Small baskets or bins
– Children's photographs

Suggested Books

– *Baby Faces* by Margaret Miller
– *The Kissing Hand* by Audrey Penn
– *My New School* by Kirsten Hall

HOW TO DO IT

Create special cubbies by personalizing them for each child. Many children's storage units are divided with places for each child's personal items. Place children's names on their cubbies, along with a current photograph of each child. Place a basket or plastic bin inside each cubby—or in a designated space if you don't have cubbies—to help you organize the children's items. As children arrive each day, show them where you place their things and which cubby belongs to them. Babies will begin to make the connection between their cubby and their own personal items, such as their favorite blanket for sleeping. Read the suggested books, introduce the vocabulary words, and sing and chant with the children.

LEARNING OUTCOMES

SOCIAL-EMOTIONAL DEVELOPMENT
– Sense of self
– Personal identity
– Relationships with adults
– Self-regulation

PHYSICAL DEVELOPMENT
– Gross-motor skills
– Fine-motor skills

COGNITIVE DEVELOPMENT
✳ Memory
✳ Following simple directions
– Spatial awareness
– Number awareness
– Imitating others

LANGUAGE DEVELOPMENT
– Receptive language
– Expressive language
– Communicating needs
– Concept words

Modifications for Twos

A good routine for two-year-olds is to have them put their things in their cubbies when they first arrive each day. When they leave, they can help their adult family members gather up their personal items. These routines provide the children with structure and help them to prepare mentally for the next part of their day. When children enter the classroom and put their things in their cubby, they know that it's time to play, explore, and learn.

Expand the Activity

Use cubbies to teach children responsibility and how to follow simple directions. For example, after a child has completed his art project, ask him to place it in his cubby. He will know it's in his cubby to take home later. Young children need opportunities to learn to follow simple directions. You can ask them to go to their cubbies and get their sweaters or jackets for outdoor play.

BUILD LANGUAGE SKILLS

Vocabulary

- Cubby
- Space
- Basket
- Mine
- Name
- Yours
- Place
- Get
- Go
- Gather
- Put

Questions and Things to Say

"Here's your cubby! It has your picture on it. See?—this is a picture of you. When we go outside later, we'll come find your cubby and get your jacket."

Song, Chants, and Fingerplays

Chant: "Welcome to School" by Kimberly Bohannon

Welcome, welcome, welcome to school!
Welcome, welcome, it's good to see you.
Welcome, welcome, let's have a great day!
Welcome, welcome, please put your things away.

Mystery Box

MATERIALS

- A shoe box or cardboard box that is deep enough to hold the objects you select
- Contact paper or wrapping paper
- A variety of familiar classroom objects

Suggested Books

- *First 100 Words* by Roger Priddy
- *It's Pumpkin Time!* by Zoe Hall
- *Where Is My Friend?* by Simms Taback

HOW TO DO IT

Cover the outside of the box and the lid with contact paper or wrapping paper. Explain how the game works by first placing an object or several like objects, such as farm animals, in the box. Hide the box in an easy-to-find location. Then search together for the mystery box. Have the child help you place another object in the box, and repeat the activity. You can include more than one child in this activity. New objects can be rotated in over time. Read the suggested books, introduce the vocabulary words, and sing and chant with the children.

Modification for Twos

As children get older, they can hide the mystery box for each other or for an adult to find. You can use this activity to reintroduce a toy or introduce new ones.

Expand the Activity

Older children can practice predicting what might be in the mystery box.

BUILD LANGUAGE SKILLS

Vocabulary

- Box
- Top
- Inside
- Hide
- Seek

- Hunt
- Locate
- Look
- See
- Find

- Found
- Shake
- Pumpkin

Questions and Things to Say

"Where shall we look for the mystery box? Shall we look under the pillow? Do you remember what was in the box? That's right—it was the pumpkin. Yay—you found it! What shall we put in the box to hide next?"

Songs, Chants, and Fingerplays

Fingerplay: "Five Little Pumpkins" by Kimberly Bohannon
(Use a small toy pumpkin in the mystery box)

Five little pumpkins growing on the vine,
One fell off and said, "I'm fine!"
Four little pumpkins growing on the vine,
One fell off and said, "It's time."
Three little pumpkins growing on the vine,
One fell off and said, "My, my!"
Two little pumpkins growing on the vine,
One fell off and said, "Good-bye!"
The last little pumpkin growing on a vine
Was picked and made into a pie. Yum, Yum! (*Say "Yum, Yum!" very slowly with a sad affect or show excitement when you say it.*)

(*As you chant, use your fingers to show the number of pumpkins. Hold your other arm up from the elbow and have your fingers "climb" from your elbow to your hand as you chant "growing on a vine."*)

The Name Game

MATERIALS

– Photographs of each child
– A mirror

Suggested Books

– *ABC I Like Me!* by Nancy Carlson
– *A to Z* by Sandra Boynton
– *Black and White Rabbit's ABC* by Alan Baker
– *Colors, ABC, Numbers* by Roger Priddy

HOW TO DO IT

Help children learn that everything has a name. Say the child's name throughout the day. Show children their photographs, and help them learn to recognize themselves in the mirror. For example, say, "Where's Maria? Here she is. Where's Maria's nose?" Show and name familiar objects to the children. Read the suggested books, introduce the vocabulary words, and sing and chant with the children.

Modifications for Twos

Help children build their vocabulary and learn the names of objects. Introduce new words and concepts to them throughout the day. As you go for a walk, play, and read with them, repeat the names of objects and encourage children to say them with you.

Expand the Activity

Select a fruit or vegetable for the children to learn about. Help them learn new vocabulary words while you describe the fruit or vegetable. Let them explore the fruit or vegetable, then cut it into smaller pieces so they can see the inside and outside of it. Let them examine and taste the fruit or vegetable, and ask them what they like and don't like about it. Let parents know what words children are learning each day so they can support the vocabulary building at home.

LEARNING OUTCOMES

SOCIAL-EMOTIONAL DEVELOPMENT
✴ Personal identity
– Sense of self
– Relationships with adults
– Relationships with peers

PHYSICAL DEVELOPMENT
– Perception
– Gross-motor skills
– Fine-motor skills

COGNITIVE DEVELOPMENT
– Memory
– Number awareness

LANGUAGE DEVELOPMENT
✴ Communicating needs
– Receptive language
– Expressive language
– Connecting words with real-world knowledge

BUILD LANGUAGE SKILLS

Vocabulary

- Mirror
- Photograph
- Baby
- Nose

- Eyes
- Mouth
- Ball
- Play

- Toy
- Read
- Book
- Apple

- Tomato
- Seeds

Questions and Things to Say

"Here's a red apple. Can you say apple with me? *Aaa-pel*. Can you point to the apple? Let's touch and smell the apple. I'm going to cut the apple and let you taste it. Look—these are the seeds. How does it taste? What do you like about the apple? Let's read *The Apple Pie Tree* book."

Songs, Chants, and Fingerplays

Song: "Where Is Maria?" by Jean Barbre
(Tune: "Frère Jacques")

Where is Maria?
Where is Maria?
Here she is.
Here she is.
We're so glad to see you.
We're so glad to see you.
Come and play.
Come and play.

One, Two, Three— Hey, That's Me!

MATERIALS

– A mirror

Suggested Books

– *ABC I Like Me!* by Nancy Carlson
– *Eyes, Nose, Fingers, and Toes: A First Book All About You* by Judy Hindley
– *Ten Little Fingers* by Annie Kubler
– *Two Eyes, a Nose, and a Mouth* by Roberta Grobel Intrater

HOW TO DO IT

Sit facing an older infant or toddler. First, verbally count and use your fingers, saying, "One, two, three." Then point and identify the different parts of the child's and your face, using the chant on the following page. The child can use a mirror to look at herself. The repetition and rhythm of the chant provide early development of sense of self and personal identity. Read the suggested books, introduce the vocabulary words, and sing and chant with the children.

Modification for Twos

Older infants and toddlers can use the chant to identify body parts. Follow the children's lead when they point out their body features. The counting of *one, two, three* provides a foundation for following simple directions. For example, "One, two, three, follow me."

Expand this Activity

As children learn to identify parts of their bodies beyond their faces, such as knees, feet, and toes, sing "Hokey Pokey" or "Head, Shoulders, Knees, and Toes."

LEARNING OUTCOMES

SOCIAL-EMOTIONAL DEVELOPMENT
* Sense of self
* Personal identity
– Relationships with adults

PHYSICAL DEVELOPMENT
– Gross-motor skills

COGNITIVE DEVELOPMENT
– Memory
– Number awareness
– Imitating others
– Progression of play

LANGUAGE DEVELOPMENT
– Receptive language
– Engaging in music, rhythm, and rhyme

BUILD LANGUAGE SKILLS

Vocabulary

- Eyes
- Ears
- Mouth
- Nose
- Chin
- Hair
- Smile
- Mirror

Questions and Things to Say

"Watch my fingers as I count one, two, three. Count with me. Let's look at your face. One, two, three, where is your nose? Here it is. Point to your nose. Now point to my nose. One, two, three, where's your mouth? One, two, three, where are your eyes?"

Songs, Chants, and Fingerplays

Chant: "One, Two, Three—Hey, That's Me!" by Jean Barbre

One, two, three, point to your mouth.
One, two, three, point to your nose.
One, two, three, point to your ears.
One, two, three—hey, that's me!"

Additional verses:
Repeat, using other parts of the body.

47

Our Special Time

MATERIALS

Suggested Books

- *How Do I Love You?* by Marion Dane Bauer
- *Mommy Hugs* by Karen Katz
- *When I Care About Others* by Cornelia Maude Spelman
- *You and Me Together: Moms, Dads, and Kids Around the World* by Barbara Kerley

HOW TO DO IT

Children need special time with their caregivers. This may be challenging when you have a large group of children, but it is important when providing high-quality child care. During the day, spend time with each child and try not to multitask. Be intentional in your interactions with every child. Look into the child's eyes and tell him how special he is to you. Find time to sit quietly with a child. Introduce the vocabulary words, and sing, chant, and read the suggested books to a child. Let all of the children know why they are special to you.

Modifications for Twos

During your special time, talk to the child about what he likes to do and what makes him special. Point out his facial features, and tell him how happy you are to have him in your classroom.

Expand the Activity

Create a bulletin board in the classroom with photos of you and other caregivers interacting with the children, enjoying special time together, reading, singing, and playing.

LEARNING OUTCOMES

SOCIAL-EMOTIONAL DEVELOPMENT
* Sense of self
- Personal identity
- Relationships with adults
- Caring for others

PHYSICAL DEVELOPMENT
- Perception

COGNITIVE DEVELOPMENT
- Spatial awareness
- Connecting experiences

LANGUAGE DEVELOPMENT
* Communicating needs
- Receptive language
- Expressive language
- Connecting words with real-world knowledge
- Engaging in print
- Using language in play

BUILD LANGUAGE SKILLS

Vocabulary

- Special
- Unique
- Beautiful
- Feel

- Loved
- Happy
- Together
- Rocking chair

- Favorite
- Friendships

Questions and Things to Say

"You are a very special child. I love being able to spend time with you. Let's read this story together as we sit in the rocking chair. I know this book is one of your favorites. It's a story about farm animals."

Songs, Chants, and Fingerplays

Song: "The More We Get Together" (traditional)

Song: "Smiling Baby" by Jean Barbre
(Tune: "Frère Jacques")

Smiling baby,
Smiling baby,
Here you are.
Here you are.
You're a special baby.
You're a special baby.
Yes, you are.
Yes, you are.

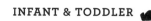

Pat-a-Cake

MATERIALS

Suggested Books

- *The Apple Pie Tree* by Zoe Hall
- *Bread, Bread, Bread* by Ann Morris
- *Curious George and the Pizza* by Margret Rey and H. A. Rey
- *Don't Touch, It's Hot* by David Algrim
- *If You Give a Mouse a Cookie* by Laura Numeroff

HOW TO DO IT

You can place older infants in your lap and allow them to lean against your stomach. Say the "Pat-a-Cake" chant, helping the child with the patting and rolling gestures. Toddlers can play this game facing you while they imitate the gestures, or they can sit in front of a mirror and chant. Read the suggested books, introduce the vocabulary words, and sing and chant with the children.

Modification for Twos

Two-year-olds can recite this chant together at circle time. The children can practice it very slowly and then quickly. Let them take turns tapping the rhythm, using a wooden spoon and a bowl.

Expand the Activity

During circle time, show photographs of people baking, and talk about what a baker does. Encourage the children to take turns acting out the role of a baker and wearing a baker's toque (white chef's hat) and apron. Place the hats and aprons in the dramatic play area.

LEARNING OUTCOMES

SOCIAL-EMOTIONAL DEVELOPMENT
- ✶ Sense of self
- – Personal identity
- – Relationships with adults

PHYSICAL DEVELOPMENT
- – Gross-motor skills

COGNITIVE DEVELOPMENT
- – Memory
- – Imitating others

LANGUAGE DEVELOPMENT
- ✶ Engaging in music, rhythm, and rhyme
- – Receptive language
- – Connecting words with real-world knowledge
- – Concept words
- – Using language in play

BUILD LANGUAGE SKILLS

Vocabulary

- Fast
- Slow
- Fist
- Throw
- Baby
- Me
- Baker
- Hat
- Cake
- Hands
- Head
- Roll
- Pat

Questions and Things to Say

"'Pat-a-Cake' is a chant about a baker. Here's a picture of a baker. He is wearing a white hat and an apron. The baker pats the dough. Patting is like clapping. We pat our hands together. Now make a fist and roll your arms in a circle. Let's recite 'Pat-a-Cake' together. Can you clap with me?"

Songs, Chants, and Fingerplays

Chant: "Pat-a-Cake" (traditional)

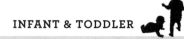

Picture Perfect

MATERIALS

– Two or four photographs of each child
– Resealable plastic bags or sheet protectors
– A hand mirror

Suggested Books

– *Eyes, Nose, Fingers, and Toes: A First Book All About You* by Judy Hindley
– *Lots of Feelings* by Shelley Rotner
– *Two Eyes, a Nose, and a Mouth* by Roberta Grobel Intrater

HOW TO DO IT

Babies and toddlers love to look at faces. Place two photographs of a child back-to-back inside a resealable bag or sheet protector. The plastic protects the photos and makes it easier for the child to handle. Show the children the pictures of themselves. Point out their eyes, noses, mouths, and ears. Encourage them to point to your facial features too. Let them see themselves in a mirror. Show them pictures of the other babies in their class too. Read the suggested books, introduce the vocabulary words, and sing and chant with the children.

Modifications for Twos

Set the photographs of two-year-olds on the floor and ask the children to pick out their own photos. Cheer them on as they pick out their pictures. Talk about what makes each child special. Say each child's name frequently during this activity.

Expand the Activity

Take photos of the babies in your classroom with a digital camera. Post the printed photos near the changing table so the babies can see them. Point out the names of the children, and talk about how special each child is to you.

LEARNING OUTCOMES

SOCIAL-EMOTIONAL DEVELOPMENT
✶ Personal identity
✶ Relationships with peers
– Sense of self
– Relationships with adults
– Empathy
– Caring for others

PHYSICAL DEVELOPMENT
– Fine-motor skills

COGNITIVE DEVELOPMENT
– Memory
– Spatial awareness
– Imitating others
– Progression of play

LANGUAGE DEVELOPMENT
– Receptive language
– Expressive language
– Using language in play

BUILD LANGUAGE SKILLS

Vocabulary

- Picture
- Face
- Eyes
- Ears
- Nose
- Mouth
- Chin
- Hair
- Mirror
- Smile
- Friend

Questions and Things to Say

"Here is a picture of you, Patrick. Here is another one of you. Look at your beautiful smile. Patrick, you are a very special baby. Can you see yourself in the mirror? Where is Patrick's nose? Can you point to it? Yes! You're right."

Songs, Chants, and Fingerplays

Song: "How Cute Is That Baby in the Mirror?" by Kimberly Bohannon
(Tune: "How Much Is That Doggie in the Window?")

How cute is that baby in the mirror?
The one with the smile on her face.
How cute is that baby in the mirror?
She's special in every way.

50

Playing with Puppets

MATERIALS

- White socks
- Scissors
- Glue
- Crayons
- Markers
- Buttons
- Pom-poms
- Yarn
- Felt
- Fabric
- Ready-made puppets

Suggested Books

- *Bear Snores On* by Karma Wilson
- *Bear's Busy Family* by Stella Blackstone
- *Harry the Dirty Dog* by Gene Zion
- *The Very Hungry Caterpillar* by Eric Carle

HOW TO DO IT

Puppets are fun for all ages. You can make a puppet or use ready-made ones when you tell a story or talk with a child. Puppets can be used to develop a sense of self in young children by fostering communication, role play, social interaction, imitation, and imagination. To make a sock puppet, take a white sock and either sew buttons on for eyes or color them in with a black marker. Decorate it using pom-poms, yarn, felt, and fabric. Use funny voices when you use the puppets to talk or read with the children. Supervise the children while they play with sturdy puppets and use them for pretend play and acting out stories. Read the suggested books and introduce the vocabulary words to the children.

Modifications for Twos

Select a story to read to the children. Find pictures on the Internet of objects in the story, such as bears, frogs, bugs, or insects. Make colored prints of the pictures. Laminate the pictures and glue them onto separate tongue depressors. Let the children hold the stick puppets while you read the story.

LEARNING OUTCOMES

SOCIAL-EMOTIONAL DEVELOPMENT
- ✱ Sense of self
- Personal identity
- Relationships with adults
- Relationships with peers
- Sharing

PHYSICAL DEVELOPMENT
- Fine-motor skills

COGNITIVE DEVELOPMENT
- Memory
- Connecting experiences
- Imitating others
- Progression of play
- Following simple directions

LANGUAGE DEVELOPMENT
- ✱ Receptive language
- Expressive language
- Communicating needs
- Engaging in print
- Using language in play

Expand the Activity

Encourage the children to create paper-bag puppets using construction paper, crayons, markers, pom-poms, yarn, felt, and fabric. Ask children to tell or retell a story using their puppets.

BUILD LANGUAGE SKILLS

Vocabulary

- Puppets
- Paper bag
- Faces
- Yarn
- Hair
- Felt
- Fabric

Questions and Things to Say

"We're going to read a story today called *Harry the Dirty Dog.* This is our puppet, Harry. He's going to go on an adventure. Let's say 'hello' to Harry."

51

Push and Pull

MATERIALS

– A variety of push-and-pull toys (such as trucks, cars, planes, balls, buggies, and shopping carts)

Suggested Books

– *ABCDrive!* by Naomi Howland
– *Dig Dig Digging* by Margaret Mayo
– *I'm Your Bus* by Marilyn Singer
– *Richard Scarry's Best First Book Ever!* by Richard Scarry

HOW TO DO IT

Provide children with a variety of large and small push-and-pull toys. Identify the name and parts of each toy. Choose toys that can be used indoors and outdoors. Make sure to include large, sturdy push-and-pull toys to stabilize children who are learning to walk and stand on their own. Children quickly learn how to play with these toys and begin to direct their own learning. Read the suggested books, introduce the vocabulary words, and sing and chant with the children.

LEARNING OUTCOMES

SOCIAL-EMOTIONAL DEVELOPMENT
– Sense of self
– Relationships with peers
– Self-regulation
– Sharing

PHYSICAL DEVELOPMENT
✳ Gross-motor skills
✳ Fine-motor skills

COGNITIVE DEVELOPMENT
– Cause and effect
– Memory
– Spatial awareness
– Connecting experiences
– Number awareness
– Progression of play
– Following simple directions

LANGUAGE DEVELOPMENT
– Receptive language
– Expressive language
– Connecting words with real-world knowledge
– Concept words
– Using language in play

Modifications for Twos

Set small toys, such as cars, trucks, and balls, in baskets or containers that are easily accessible for play in all the learning centers. Model how children can incorporate these toys with other play materials. For example, help the children build ramps out of blocks and show them how they can roll and push the cars up and down the ramps.

Expand the Activity

Model how toys with baskets, such as shopping carts or wagons, can be used to carry items from one area to another. This stimulates children's imaginations and develops number and spatial awareness. Read the suggested books, and talk about the different types of jobs of people who drive cars and trucks.

BUILD LANGUAGE SKILLS

Vocabulary

- Push
- Pull
- Over
- Under
- Carry
- Move
- Trucks
- Cars
- Shopping cart
- Wagon
- Buggy

Questions and Things to Say

"Look at you walking! You can push the buggy around the room. What toys should we put in the buggy? Can you put the cars in the buggy and take them to the block area?"

Songs, Chants, and Fingerplays

Song: "Push and Pull" by Kimberly Bohannon
(Tune: "Deep and Wide")

Push and pull.
Push and pull.
We can push and pull, fast and slow.

Push and pull.
Push and pull.
We can push and pull, in and out.

Push and pull.
Push and pull.
We can push and pull, back and forth.

52

Ready, Set, Read

MATERIALS

- A variety of books
- Baskets

Suggested Books

- *Actual Size* by Steve Jenkins
- *Annie, Bea, and Chi Chi Dolores: A School Day Alphabet* by Donna Maurer
- *Brown Bear, Brown Bear, What Do You See?* by Bill Martin Jr.
- *Click, Clack, Quackity-Quack: An Alphabetical Adventure* by Doreen Cronin
- *First 100 Words* by Roger Priddy
- *The Grouchy Ladybug* by Eric Carle
- *Lola at the Library* by Anna McQuinn and Rosalind Beardshaw
- *Read and Rise* by Sandra L. Pinkney
- *Richard Scarry's Best First Book Ever!* by Richard Scarry

HOW TO DO IT

Place a variety of books in baskets or containers throughout your indoor and outdoor space. Give babies and young toddlers chunky and soft cloth books. Books should include rhyming, counting, letter and number awareness, and familiar objects. You'll also want books that help children learn about their feelings and getting along with others. Reading to children helps build your relationship with them. Use this opportunity to ask children questions about the stories. Being read to helps children develop receptive and expressive language skills. Rotate a few new books into the baskets each week to increase children's interest. Leave their favorite books in the baskets. Read the suggested books, introduce the vocabulary words, and sing and chant with the children.

LEARNING OUTCOMES

SOCIAL-EMOTIONAL DEVELOPMENT
✳ Relationships with adults
- Sense of self
- Personal identity
- Relationships with peers
- Self-regulation
- Empathy
- Caring for others
- Sharing

PHYSICAL DEVELOPMENT
- Fine-motor skills

COGNITIVE DEVELOPMENT
- Cause and effect
- Memory
- Spatial awareness
- Connecting experiences
- Number awareness
- Following simple directions

LANGUAGE DEVELOPMENT
✳ Engaging in print
- Receptive language
- Expressive language
- Communicating needs
- Connecting words with real-world knowledge
- Concept words
- Engaging in music, rhythm, and rhyme

Modifications for Twos

Older children can follow more complex stories. They will enjoy reading books that rhyme and ones with repeating lines they can recite to you, such as *Brown Bear, Brown Bear, What Do You See?* Children love to have their favorite stories read and reread to them.

Expand the Activity

Use puppets and felt stories to bring a new dimension to a book.

BUILD LANGUAGE SKILLS

Vocabulary

- Book
- Author
- Illustrator
- Cover
- Back
- Puppets
- Felt
- Other words that are found in the books

Questions and Things to Say

"Reading books is fun. We can learn a lot about the world through books. What book shall we read today? Here's a book about dogs and cats. Do any of you have a dog or cat at home? Let's read the story with our dog puppet."

Songs, Chants, and Fingerplays

Song: "Pick a Book" by Kimberly Bohannon (Tune: "Three Blind Mice")

Time to read.
Time to read.
Pick a book.
Pick a book.
Read about cats and dogs.
Trains, boats, and frogs.
Let's pick a book.
Pick a book.

Rock and Roll

MATERIALS

Suggested Books

– *ABC I Like Me!* by Nancy Carlson
– *I'm Your Bus* by Marilyn Singer
– *Mama Zooms* by Jane Cowen-Fletcher
– *You and Me Together: Moms, Dads, and Kids Around the World* by Barbara Kerley

HOW TO DO IT

Babies love to be gently bounced and rocked. Lay a baby across your thighs, supporting her head, and gently rock her from side to side. You can also do this as part of tummy time to help babies develop their stomach muscles. You can lift your thighs up one at a time, as if you are marching, when you play with toddlers. This gives them a bumping experience. Read the suggested books, introduce the vocabulary words, and sing and chant with the children.

Modifications for Twos

Children can sit on your lap and be bounced gently up and down. You might want to sing a song, such as "Pat-a-Cake," to keep the beat while you bump the children up and down on your lap. Help children develop concept words by describing the actions, such as moving up and down and being lifted high and low.

Expand the Activity

Seat a child on your lap and move your arms and legs as you sing a song. Read the book *I'm Your Bus* and then sing "The Wheels on the Bus" and teach the children the motions.

LEARNING OUTCOMES

SOCIAL-EMOTIONAL DEVELOPMENT
– Sense of self
– Relationships with adults

PHYSICAL DEVELOPMENT
✱ Gross-motor skills

COGNITIVE DEVELOPMENT
✱ Connecting experiences
– Spatial awareness

LANGUAGE DEVELOPMENT
– Receptive language
– Expressive language
– Communicating needs
– Connecting words with real-world knowledge
– Concept words
– Engaging in music, rhythm, and rhyme

BUILD LANGUAGE SKILLS

Vocabulary

- Bump
- Rock
- Swing
- Move
- Roll

- Up
- Down
- Back
- Forth
- High

- Low
- Wheels
- Bus

Questions and Things to Say

"I'm rubbing your back as I rock you side to side. Now you're moving slowly up and down. Can you feel yourself moving up and down? You are being lifted high off the ground. It's fun to move our bodies this way."

Songs, Chants, and Fingerplays

Song: "Rock-a-Bye Baby" (traditional)

Song: "The Wheels on the Bus" (traditional)

Chant: "Moving Time" by Kimberly Bohannon

Up and down,
Up and down,
Let's move our bodies
Up and down.

Side to side,
Side to side,
Let's roll our bodies
Side to side.

Left and right,
Left and right,
Let's move our bodies
Left and right.

Back and forth,
Back and forth,
Let's rock our bodies
Back and forth.

Round About

MATERIALS

- Wood blocks
- A medium-size box
- An assortment of different-size, too-large-to-be-swallowed round and circular objects (such as balls, stacking rings, cups, and bottles)

Suggested Books

- *ABCDrive!* by Naomi Howland
- *Dig Dig Digging* by Margaret Mayo
- *Gray Rabbit's Odd One Out* by Alan Baker
- *Opposites* by Sandra Boynton

HOW TO DO IT

Show children the round objects in the box and begin to describe them. Encourage the children to feel the objects and roll them on the table or floor. Use wood blocks to create a ramp for items to roll down. Read the suggested books, introduce the vocabulary words, and sing and chant with the children.

Modifications for Twos

Encourage older children to search the room for round objects and then have them sort the objects by size from smallest to largest. Go for a walk outdoors and point out all the things that are round, such as door knobs, tires, flowerpots, and trash cans. Read suggested books to the children.

Expand the Activity

Using paper, crayons, and markers, encourage older children to trace around larger circular objects. Older children can practice drawing circles with chalk on the pavement outdoors.

LEARNING OUTCOMES

SOCIAL-EMOTIONAL DEVELOPMENT
- Relationships with adults
- Sharing

PHYSICAL DEVELOPMENT
- Perception
- Fine-motor skills

COGNITIVE DEVELOPMENT
∗ Spatial awareness
∗ Connecting experiences
- Cause and effect
- Memory
- Imitating others
- Progression of play

LANGUAGE DEVELOPMENT
- Receptive language
- Expressive language
- Connecting words with real-world knowledge
- Concept words
- Using language in play

BUILD LANGUAGE SKILLS

Vocabulary

- Round
- Roll
- Bounce
- Ball

- Rings
- Bottle tops
- Small
- Large

- Circle
- Chalk

Questions and Things to Say

"Let's look carefully at the toys that are round. Let's watch them roll and bounce. Where are the round objects outside? Let's look!"

Songs, Chants, and Fingerplays

Chant: "Roll It" by Kimberly Bohannon

Roll it,
Roll it,
Roll it to me,
Roll it to me as fast as can be.

Scarf Dance

MATERIALS

- A shoe box or cardboard box with a lid
- Contact paper
- Wrapping paper
- Scissors
- Glue
- Scarves of different colors, textures, and patterns or large pieces of fabric

Suggested Books

- *Barnyard Dance!* by Sandra Boynton
- *Giraffes Can't Dance* by Giles Andreae
- *Rosie's Walk* by Pat Hutchins

HOW TO DO IT

Cut a hole in the top of the box large enough to pull the scarves through. Cover the box with contact paper or wrapping paper. Place the scarves inside the cardboard box. Slowly pull them out one at a time. Identify the color, texture, and pattern of each scarf. Let the children take turns feeling the different textures. Everyone can swing the scarves around their heads, through their legs, and behind their backs. Fabric pieces can be substituted for the scarves. You can hold the babies as they do this activity. Read the suggested books, introduce the vocabulary words, and sing and chant with the children.

Modifications for Twos

Two-year-olds can take turns pulling the scarves out of the box. During small-group time, verbalize concept words such as *under*, *over*, *around*, and *through* while the children play with the scarves. Play music while they dance and move with the scarves.

LEARNING OUTCOMES

SOCIAL-EMOTIONAL DEVELOPMENT
- Sense of self
- Relationships with adults
- Relationships with peers
- Sharing

PHYSICAL DEVELOPMENT
- ✴ Gross-motor skills
- Perception
- Fine-motor skills

COGNITIVE DEVELOPMENT
- ✴ Progression of play
- Memory
- Spatial awareness
- Connecting experiences
- Imitating others

LANGUAGE DEVELOPMENT
- Receptive language
- Expressive language
- Concept words
- Engaging in music, rhythm, and rhyme
- Using language in play

Expand the Activity

Older children can practice predicting what scarf will be pulled out next. Ask them questions about the patterns, colors, and textures of the scarves. Scarves can also be used in the dramatic play area.

BUILD LANGUAGE SKILLS

Vocabulary

- Scarf
- Smooth
- Silky
- Shiny
- Pattern

- Design
- Under
- Over
- Around
- Through

- Up
- Down
- Color words

Questions and Things to Say

"See the scarves. How does this scarf feel? Is it smooth and shiny? What colors do you see in the design? What patterns do you see? What happens when I throw the scarf up in the air? What scarf should we pull out of the box next?"

Songs, Chants, and Fingerplays

Chant: "What Scarves Can Do" by Kimberly Bohannon

Shiny, smooth, colorful too.
Let's see what our scarves can do!
Shake and move your scarf around,
Swing it high and near the ground.
Shake and toss it in the air,
Watch it float and land somewhere.
Shiny, smooth, colorful too.
What did you see your scarf do?

56

Sensing Something Different

MATERIALS

- A small, sturdy box or shoe box
- Materials with different textures (such as sandpaper, plastic wrap, doubled-sided tape, fake fur, felt, and bubble wrap)
- Scissors
- Electrical tape
- Markers
- Contact paper
- Glue

Suggested Books

- *Don't Touch, It's Hot* by David Algrim
- *First 100 Words* by Roger Priddy
- *My Five Senses* by Aliki
- *My Five Senses* by Margaret Miller
- *Where Is My Friend?* by Simms Taback

HOW TO DO IT

Lay the materials out on a table. Let the children feel them, and explain how each has a different texture. Help children learn the names of the different materials. Then cut a hole in the top of the box large enough for a child's hand. Cover the edges of the hole with electrical tape. Use glue to line the inside of the box with the textured materials. Cover the outside of the box with contact paper. Use a marker to label the box "Sensory Box." Let children take turns feeling inside the box. Ask them what they feel and what they like and dislike about the textures. Read the suggested books, introduce the vocabulary words, and sing and chant with the children.

LEARNING OUTCOMES

SOCIAL-EMOTIONAL DEVELOPMENT
- ✱ Sharing
- Sense of self
- Relationships with adults
- Relationships with peers

PHYSICAL DEVELOPMENT
- ✱ Perception
- Fine-motor skills

COGNITIVE DEVELOPMENT
- Cause and effect
- Memory
- Spatial awareness
- Connecting experiences
- Imitating others
- Progression of play
- Following simple directions

LANGUAGE DEVELOPMENT
- Receptive language
- Expressive language
- Connecting words with real-world knowledge
- Concept words
- Using language in play

Modifications for Twos

Shine a flashlight through the hole. Let the children peek at the different sides of the sensory box and tell you what they see.

Expand the Activity

Go for a walk outdoors and collect materials that can be used for a another sensory box.

BUILD LANGUAGE SKILLS

Vocabulary

- Box
- Top
- Bottom
- Hole

- Touch
- Feel
- Smooth
- Texture

- Sandpaper
- Rough
- Soft
- Sticky

- Fur
- Hands
- Fingers
- Senses

Questions and Things to Say

"We're going to create a sensory box. Here are several different textures for you to feel. This piece is called sandpaper. It feels rough. How is it different from the fur? Which texture feels sticky?"

Songs, Chants, and Fingerplays

Song: "The Textures in the Box" by Jean Barbre
(Tune: "The Wheels on the Bus")

The textures in the box are
Rough and smooth,
Rough and smooth,
Rough and smooth.
The textures in the box are
rough and smooth.
See how they feel?

(Repeat song with other textures.)

Shell It Out

MATERIALS

– Up to three small- to medium-size opaque storage containers
– Toys or object small enough to fit under the containers

Suggested Books

– *Bugs! Bugs! Bugs!* by Bob Barner
– *Little Rabbits' First Farm Book* by Alan Baker
– *On the Seashore* by Anna Milborne
– *Way Down Deep in the Deep Blue Sea* by Jan Peck

HOW TO DO IT

Show the children a toy or object, and then place the item under the container. Lift the container up and look surprised when you see the object. Identify it by name. Repeat the activity, encouraging the children to lift up the container to find the toy. Then add a second container, and move the toy between the two containers. Read the suggested books, introduce the vocabulary words, and sing and chant with the children.

Modifications for Twos

Children can engage in this activity by hiding the toy from you. They will delight in tricking you.

Expand the Activity

You can use three different-size containers for older children and one or two toys. Encourage children to play this game together.

LEARNING OUTCOMES

SOCIAL-EMOTIONAL DEVELOPMENT
– Sense of self
– Relationships with adults
– Self-regulation

PHYSICAL DEVELOPMENT
– Fine-motor skills

COGNITIVE DEVELOPMENT
✱ Memory
✱ Spatial awareness
– Cause and effect
– Connecting experiences
– Number awareness
– Imitating others
– Progression of play

LANGUAGE DEVELOPMENT
– Receptive language

BUILD LANGUAGE SKILLS

Vocabulary

- Container
- Under
- Big

- Little
- Lift
- Hide

- Find
- Look
- See

Questions and Things to Say

"I'm going to place this seashell under the tub. Where did it go? Let's see what happens when we lift the container up. Can you see it now? Shall we put it under the tub again? You try it. Here's another container. Which tub is it under?"

Songs, Chants, and Fingerplays

Song: "Where Is It?"
by Kimberly Bohannon
(Tune: "Frère Jacques")

Let's remember,
Let's remember,
Where it is,
Where it is.
Is it under here?
Is it under here?
Where is it?
Where is it?

Variation if using more than one box:
Let's remember,
Let's remember,
Where it is,
Where it is.
Is it under here?
Or is it under there?
Where is it?
Where is it?

Sitting Pretty

MATERIALS

Suggested Books

- *Eyes, Nose, Fingers, and Toes: A First Book All About You* by Judy Hindley
- *Here Are My Hands* by Bill Martin Jr. and John Archambault
- *Mama Zooms* by Jane Cowen-Fletcher
- *Two Eyes, a Nose, and a Mouth* by Roberta Grobel Intrater

HOW TO DO IT

Once babies can safely hold up their heads, you can begin to play this game. Place the baby or toddler flat on her back resting on a soft rug or pillow. Hold onto the baby's hands and wrists and count, "One, two, three, sit up with me!" while gently pulling her to a sitting position. Children love anticipating this activity and will giggle and laugh when you encourage them to sit up. Read the suggested books, introduce the vocabulary words, and sing and chant with the children.

Modifications for Twos

Provide children with furniture and toys to crawl over and under and push-and-pull toys to practice walking.

Expand the Activity

Provide low furniture so older infants can practice pulling themselves up. Use your hands to help crawling children to standing positions. Hold their hands while they practice walking.

LEARNING OUTCOMES

SOCIAL-EMOTIONAL DEVELOPMENT
* Relationships with adults
- Sense of self

PHYSICAL DEVELOPMENT
* Gross-motor skills

COGNITIVE DEVELOPMENT
- Memory
- Connecting experiences
- Number awareness
- Progression of play

LANGUAGE DEVELOPMENT
- Receptive language
- Concept words
- Engaging in music, rhythm, and rhyme

BUILD LANGUAGE SKILLS

Vocabulary

- Sit
- Sitting
- Up
- Crawl
- Climb
- Walk
- Run
- Hand
- Hold

Questions and Things to Say

"We're going to practice sitting up. I'm going to hold your hands and count to three. Here we go!"

Songs, Chants, and Fingerplays

Song: "Sitting Pretty"
by Kimberly Bohannon
(Tune: "Frère Jacques")

Sitting pretty,
Sitting pretty,
Look at me,
Look at me!
I am sitting up now,
I am sitting up now,
Look at me!
Look at me!

Crawling, crawling,
Crawling, crawling,
Here I go,
Here I go!

I am busy crawling,
I am busy crawling,
Watch me go!
Watch me go!

Song: "Push and Pull"
by Kimberly Bohannon
(Tune: "Deep and Wide")

Push and pull,
Push and pull,
We can push and pull, fast and slow.

Push and pull,
Push and pull,
We can push and pull, in and out.

Push and pull,
Push and pull,
We can push and pull, back and forth.

Stack and Tumble

MATERIALS

– Soft, stackable blocks

Suggested Books

– *A to Z* by Sandra Boynton
– *Opposites* by Sandra Boynton
– *Richard Scarry's Best First Book Ever!*
  by Richard Scarry
– *Richard Scarry's What Do People Do All Day?*
  by Richard Scarry

HOW TO DO IT

On a flat surface, model how to stack the soft
blocks. Begin by stacking a few yourself. Assist the
children in stacking their blocks next to yours.
Comment on the blocks' height as you add two or
three blocks to your tower. Animate your response
when the children knock over the tower of blocks.
Invite them to build their own towers and repeat
the tumbling activity. Talk to them about the
importance of knocking over only their own towers.
If they accidently knock over someone else's, ask
them to help rebuild it and remind them to say they're sorry. Read the suggested books,
introduce the vocabulary words, and sing and chant with the children.

Modifications for Twos

Encourage older children to build a tower together, taking turns putting on the next block.
Older children can use cardboard blocks for building.

Expand the Activity

With the children, count the number of blocks they are stacking. Ask several groups of
children to build their own towers to see which group can stack the tallest one.

LEARNING OUTCOMES

SOCIAL-EMOTIONAL DEVELOPMENT
* Self-regulation
– Sense of self
– Relationships with adults
– Relationships with peers
– Caring for others
– Sharing

PHYSICAL DEVELOPMENT
– Perception
– Gross-motor skills
– Fine-motor skills

COGNITIVE DEVELOPMENT
* Imitating others
– Cause and effect
– Memory
– Spatial awareness
– Progression of play

LANGUAGE DEVELOPMENT
– Receptive language
– Expressive language
– Communicating needs
– Concept words
– Using language in play

BUILD LANGUAGE SKILLS

Vocabulary

- Soft
- Blocks
- Build
- Tower

- Tumble
- Count
- High
- Low

- Up
- Down
- Tall
- Short

- Big
- Little

Questions and Things to Say

"Will you help me stack a tower? How high do you think we can build it? Count the number of blocks with me: one, two, three. Do you think it will tumble over? Oops—there it goes!"

Songs, Chants, and Fingerplays

Chant: "I've Built a Block Tower"
by Kimberly Bohannon

I've built a block tower
That's big and tall.
I'm knocking mine over
And watching it fall.

I'll build it again,
As tall as can be,
We'll build it together,
Just you and me.

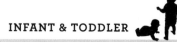

60

Straight Out of the Box

MATERIALS

– Medium to large cardboard shipping boxes

Suggested Books

– *Big Earth, Little Me* by Thom Wiley
– *Chicka Chicka Boom Boom* by Bill Martin Jr. and John Archambault
– *The Cleanup Surprise* by Christine Loomis
– *Not a Box* by Antoinette Portis
– *Too Many Toys* by David Shannon

HOW TO DO IT

Select a cardboard box for the children to use. Medium-size boxes are easier for older babies and young toddlers. Older toddlers can more easily use larger shipping boxes. Babies will enjoy sitting in a medium-size box and may explore it with their mouths. Place pillows, soft toys, and books in the box for children to use. As babies get older, they will learn to climb in and out of the box. If you open up the bottom and place the box on its side, babies can practice crawling through it and play peekaboo with you. Always supervise children who are playing with boxes; never let them feel stuck while playing inside. Help them take turns playing with the box. Read the suggested books and introduce the vocabulary words to the children.

Modifications for Twos

Create cutouts and peekaboo spaces in large cardboard boxes for two-year-olds to use. Children can select favorite books and objects to place in the box. Model how they can use markers to decorate the inside and outside.

LEARNING OUTCOMES

SOCIAL-EMOTIONAL DEVELOPMENT
– Sense of self
– Personal identity
– Relationships with adults
– Sharing

PHYSICAL DEVELOPMENT
– Gross-motor skills
– Fine-motor skills

COGNITIVE DEVELOPMENT
✶ Progression of play
– Cause and effect
– Memory
– Spatial awareness
– Connecting experiences
– Imitating others

LANGUAGE DEVELOPMENT
✶ Using language in play
– Receptive language
– Expressive language
– Concept words
– Engaging in print

Expand the Activity

You can support children's imaginative use of boxes by reading about transforming the boxes into objects, such as trucks, trains, or boats. Use electrical tape to connect two or three large, open boxes together into a tunnel for the children to explore.

BUILD LANGUAGE SKILLS

Vocabulary

- Box
- Cardboard
- Brown
- Play
- Imagination
- Explore
- Climb
- In
- Out
- Inside
- Outside
- Walls
- Markers
- Decorate
- Open
- Closed

Questions and Things to Say

"We're going to explore a cardboard box today. I'm going to open it up and let you climb into and out of it. Look at you, sitting in the box! Would you like to have some toys to play with in there?"

Tapping to the Tune

MATERIALS

- Instrumental music
- Tom-tom drum
- Rhythm sticks
- Tambourines
- Maracas
- Sandpaper blocks
- Other rhythm instruments

Suggested Books

- *Here Are My Hands* by Bill Martin Jr. and John Archambault
- *Mouse's First Day of School* by Lauren Thompson
- *Zin! Zin! Zin! A Violin* by Lloyd Moss

HOW TO DO IT

Let children select a musical instrument to use. These can be homemade or purchased. Play a song with a slow rhythm and beat, and demonstrate how you use the instruments to keep the beat of the music. Repeat the song, and ask the children to join you in keeping rhythm to the music. Don't worry if they can't—they will enjoy just playing with the musical instruments and being part of the activity. You can hold infants and toddlers on your lap and guide their hands while tapping or shaking the musical instruments. Read the suggested books, introduce the vocabulary words, and sing and chant with the children.

Modifications for Twos

In a small group or during circle time, ask the children to take turns playing an instrument and passing it to the child next to them.

LEARNING OUTCOMES

SOCIAL-EMOTIONAL DEVELOPMENT
* Sharing
- Sense of self
- Relationships with adults
- Relationships with peers
- Self-regulation

PHYSICAL DEVELOPMENT
- Perception
- Fine-motor skills

COGNITIVE DEVELOPMENT
- Cause and effect
- Memory
- Spatial awareness
- Connecting experiences
- Imitating others
- Progression of play

LANGUAGE DEVELOPMENT
* Engaging in music, rhythm, and rhyme
- Receptive language
- Expressive language
- Connecting words with real-world knowledge
- Concept words

Expand the Activity

Have children make their own musical instruments, such as tom-toms, maracas, and tambourines. See activity 98, Tom-Tom Drum.

BUILD LANGUAGE SKILLS

Vocabulary

- Tap
- Tapping
- Shake
- Drum
- Maracas
- Tambourine
- Rhythm
- Beat

Questions and Things to Say

"Music has a beat. Listen while I tap to the beat of this song. Join me in tapping or shaking your instruments. How do our instruments sound different from each other?"

Songs, Chants, and Fingerplays

Chant: "Marching Beat"
by Kimberly Bohannon

Keep the rhythm,
Yes, keep the beat,
March around
And move your feet.
Keep the rhythm,
Yes, keep the beat,
Play your drum,
And move your feet.

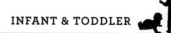

This Little Light of Mine

MATERIALS

– Incandescent lamps

Suggested Books

– *Harold and the Purple Crayon* by Crockett Johnson
– *The Very Lonely Firefly* by Eric Carle
– *What Will the Weather Be Like Today?*
  by Paul Rogers

HOW TO DO IT

Show infants and toddlers how lights go on and off. Using an incandescent lamp, demonstrate how to turn the light on and off. Show the children other types of lighting in the classroom. Talk about how the sun gives the room light too. Explain that when it's dark, we need light to help us see. Describe how people typically sleep in rooms where the light is off or dim. Read the suggested books, introduce the vocabulary words, and sing and chant with the children.

Modifications for Twos

Show children other objects that help us see in the dark, such as flashlights, lanterns, and candles. Walk outdoors and show the children outdoor lighting.

Expand the Activity

Show the children a flashlight and how to turn it on and off. Flash the light on the floor, and ask the children to follow it with their eyes. Next, shine it on the floor, and ask the children to stand on it. Move the light to another spot on the floor, and ask them to move again. Shine the light on the ceiling, and watch the children's expressions. Ask them, "Where did the light go?" Shine the light on a new spot in the room. Remember to explain to the children not to shine a light in someone's eyes.

LEARNING OUTCOMES

SOCIAL-EMOTIONAL DEVELOPMENT
– Sense of self
– Relationships with adults
– Relationships with peers
– Sharing

PHYSICAL DEVELOPMENT
– Perception
– Gross-motor skills

COGNITIVE DEVELOPMENT
✳ Cause and effect
✳ Imitating others
– Memory
– Spatial awareness
– Connecting experiences
– Progression of play
– Following simple directions

LANGUAGE DEVELOPMENT
– Receptive language
– Expressive language
– Connecting words with
  real-world knowledge
– Concept words
– Engaging in print
– Using language in play

BUILD LANGUAGE SKILLS

Vocabulary

- Light
- Dark
- On
- Off
- Dim
- Lamp
- Lightbulb
- See
- Which
- Flashlight
- Inside
- Outside
- Lantern
- Streetlight

Questions and Things to Say

"Light helps us see. The sun gives us light, and so do lamps and flashlights. Let's look outdoors and see what kind of lights you can find outside. Do you see this light next to the door? Watch while I turn it on. What happens?"

Songs, Chants, and Fingerplays

Song: "On and Off" by Kimberly Bohannon
(Tune: "Deep and Wide")

On and off,
On and off,
We can turn the light switch
On and off.
On and off.

On and off,
On and off,
We can turn the flashlight
On and off.
On and off.

On and off,
On and off,
We can turn the lightbulb
On and off.
On and off.

Song: "You Are My Sunshine" (traditional)

Twist and Twirl

MATERIALS

– Instrumental music with slow and fast tempos

Suggested Books

– *Barnyard Dance!* by Sandra Boynton
– *Dancing Feet!* by Lindsey Craig
– *Giraffes Can't Dance* by Giles Andreae
– *Hippos Go Berserk!* by Sandra Boynton

HOW TO DO IT

Describe and demonstrate to the children how to twist and twirl their bodies. You may first want to twirl a younger child under your arm or help them learn to twirl on their own. When they are ready to twirl, turn on the music and encourage them to twist and twirl their bodies. Alternate the tempo and beat of the music so children can move slowly or quickly depending on the beat. Be sure to allow enough space between children so they don't bump into each other. Adults can hold and move with babies while participating in this activity. Describe to the babies what you're doing. Read the suggested books, introduce the vocabulary words, and sing and chant with the children.

Modifications for Twos

Allow older children to pick out their favorite songs to play, and ask them to guess if the music will be fast or slow.

Expand the Activity

At circle time, ask a child to pick a friend to dance with while the rest of the children watch and clap to the music. Repeat so every child has a turn.

LEARNING OUTCOMES

SOCIAL-EMOTIONAL DEVELOPMENT
– Sense of self
– Relationships with adults
– Relationships with peers
– Self-regulation
– Sharing

PHYSICAL DEVELOPMENT
✱ Gross-motor skills

COGNITIVE DEVELOPMENT
✱ Imitating others
– Cause and effect
– Spatial awareness
– Connecting experiences
– Progression of play
– Following simple directions

LANGUAGE DEVELOPMENT
– Receptive language
– Expressive language
– Communicating needs
– Connecting words with real-world knowledge
– Concept words
– Engaging in music, rhythm, and rhyme

BUILD LANGUAGE SKILLS

Vocabulary

- Twist
- Twirl
- Turn
- Beat
- Clap
- Music
- Fast
- Slow
- Bump
- Neighbor

Questions and Things to Say

"Twisting and twirling is fun to do. Watch me while I twist to the music. I'm going to turn on the fast music, and we can twist and turn to it. Be careful not to bump into your neighbor. Join me in twisting and turning to the music."

Songs, Chants, and Fingerplays

Chant: "Twist and Twirl" by Kimberly Bohannon

Get your body movin',
Get your body groovin',
And twist and twirl,
And twist and twirl.

Twist your body fast,
Twist your body slow,
And twist and twirl,
And twist and twirl.

Twirl to the left,
Twirl to the right,
And twist and twirl,
And twist and twirl.

Get your body movin',
Get your body groovin',
And twist and twirl,
And twist and twirl.

We Go Together

MATERIALS

– A variety of items that go together or match (such as socks and shoes, mittens and hats, measuring spoons, and a pail and shovel)

Suggested Books

– *On the Seashore* by Anna Milborne and Erica-Jane Waters
– *Richard Scarry's Best First Book Ever!* by Richard Scarry
– *Richard Scarry's What Do People Do All Day?* by Richard Scarry
– *Rosie's Walk* by Pat Hutchins
– *A Sock Is a Pocket for Your Toes: A Pocket Book* by Elizabeth Garton Scanlon
– *Some Things Go Together* by Charlotte Zolotow

HOW TO DO IT

Share with children how some items go together. Show the items you have selected, and talk about what goes with what and why. When reading stories, show pictures of things that go together. When children are playing, point out things that go together—for example, paint and paintbrushes, puzzle boards and puzzle pieces, and wheels and cars. Read the suggested books, introduce the vocabulary words, and sing and chant with the children.

Modifications for Twos

Collect a variety of items and help the children sort items that go together. Tell then that there can be more than two items that go together—for example, a boat, a fishing pole, a bucket, and a fish.

LEARNING OUTCOMES

SOCIAL-EMOTIONAL DEVELOPMENT
– Sense of self
– Relationships with adults
– Relationships with peers
– Sharing

PHYSICAL DEVELOPMENT
– Perception
– Fine-motor skills

COGNITIVE DEVELOPMENT
– Memory
– Spatial awareness
– Connecting experiences
– Number awareness
– Imitating others

LANGUAGE DEVELOPMENT
✳ Receptive language
✳ Expressive language
– Connecting words with real-world knowledge
– Concept words

Expand the Activity

Before you read a story to the children, ask them to share what things might go with the story. For example, when you're reading *On the Seashore*, the children might mention seashells, sand, water, and birds.

BUILD LANGUAGE SKILLS

Vocabulary

- Together
- Match
- Like
- Different
- Same

Questions and Things to Say

"I'm going to put some things on the rug, and we're going to talk about what goes together. What goes with the hat? You're right—mittens go with the hat. We wear our hat and mittens together when it's cold outside. What about our shoes? What do we wear with them? Our socks—that's right. They go together."

Songs, Chants, and Fingerplays

Song: "What Goes Together" by Kimberly Bohannon
(Tune: "The More We Get Together")

Let's find what goes together,
Together, together.
Let's find what goes together,
Let's look for a match.

Does this go
With that thing?
Does that go
With this thing?
Let's find what goes together,
Let's look for a match.

65

Whatever Floats Your Boat

MATERIALS

- Plastic tub
- Water
- Items that will sink and float (such as a cork, feather, rock, rubber ducky, domino, pencil, piece of straw, or yarn)
- Bumpy plastic ball or sensory ball

Suggested Books

- *Bubbles, Bubbles* by Kathi Appelt
- *First 100 Words* by Roger Priddy
- *My Five Senses* by Aliki
- *My Five Senses* by Margaret Miller
- *On the Seashore* by Anna Milborne
- *Opposites* by Sandra Boynton

HOW TO DO IT

Note: This activity is designed for older infants and toddlers. Remember: never leave a child alone near or in the water.

First, let the older infant or toddler play and explore with the objects. Then fill a plastic tub with 4 to 6 inches of water. Select three to five toys that float or sink. Describe the surface and texture of the objects. Introduce the floating ones first, and then the heavier ones. Use concept words while you describe the activity. Read the suggested books, introduce the vocabulary words, and sing and chant with the children.

Modification for Twos

Encourage older children to search through the room for new toys or objects to test for sinking or floating. Two or three toddlers can take turns playing with the toys and observing if they sink or float.

LEARNING OUTCOMES

SOCIAL-EMOTIONAL DEVELOPMENT
- Personal identity
- Relationships with adults
- Relationships with peers
- Sharing

PHYSICAL DEVELOPMENT
- Perception
- Gross-motor skills
- Fine-motor skills

COGNITIVE DEVELOPMENT
- Cause and effect
- Memory
- Spatial awareness
- Connecting experiences
- Imitating others
- Progression of play
- Following simple directions

LANGUAGE DEVELOPMENT
- ✷ Connecting words with real-world knowledge
- ✷ Concept words
- Receptive language
- Expressive language
- Engaging in print
- Engaging in music, rhythm, and rhyme

Expand the Activity

Ask children to predict if the objects will sink or float. Place a small, flat boat in the water. Let the children take turns placing pennies in the boat to see how many it can hold before it sinks.

BUILD LANGUAGE SKILLS

Vocabulary

- Light
- Heavy
- Float
- Sink
- Slippery
- Wet
- Splash
- Rock
- Feather
- Cork
- Domino
- Straw
- Yarn
- Fast
- Slow

Questions and Things to Say

"Some things are heavy and some are light. Let's see what happens when we place different objects in the water. What do you think will happen when we place the cork in the water? Will it float or sink? What happens when we put the domino in the water? Do you think we can put more than one item in the water? Let's see what happens."

Songs, Chants, and Fingerplays

Song: "Sink or Float"
by Kimberly Bohannon
(Tune: "Deep and Wide")

Sink or float,
Sink or float,
Let's see if our toys sink
Or float!

Sink or float,
Sink or float,
Let's see if our toys sink
Or float!

Chant: "In the Water"
by Kimberly Bohannon

Put it in the water,
See where it goes.
Does it stay on top
Or fall down below?

Put it in the water,
See where it goes.
Does it float on top
Or sink down below?

Alphabet Soup

MATERIALS

- One 49-ounce can of low-sodium chicken or vegetable broth
- Two 8-ounce bags of alphabet pasta or other small pasta
- Cookie sheet
- Bag of frozen mixed vegetables
- Salt
- Pepper
- Heavy saucepan
- Hot plate or stove
- Large wooden or metal spoon
- Small bowls
- Spoons

Suggested Books

- *ABCDrive!* by Naomi Howland
- *Chicka Chicka Boom Boom* by Bill Martin Jr. and John Archambault
- *Growing Vegetable Soup* by Lois Ehlert

HOW TO DO IT

Place one bag of uncooked alphabet pasta on a cookie sheet. Let the children play with and examine the letters. Describe the shapes of the letters. Use them to form simple words, including the children's names. At circle time, read the story *Growing Vegetable Soup*. Show the children the items you'll be putting into the alphabet soup. Pour all ingredients into the saucepan. Let the children take turns stirring the soup before you place it on the heat. Cook on medium heat and serve. Read the suggested books, introduce the vocabulary words, and sing and chant with the children.

LEARNING OUTCOMES

SOCIAL-EMOTIONAL DEVELOPMENT
- Sense of self
- Relationships with adults
- Relationships with peers
- Sharing

PHYSICAL DEVELOPMENT
- Perception
- Fine-motor skills

COGNITIVE DEVELOPMENT
✱ Following simple directions
- Cause and effect
- Memory
- Spatial awareness
- Connecting experiences
- Number awareness
- Imitating others
- Progression of play

LANGUAGE DEVELOPMENT
✱ Using language in play
- Receptive language
- Expressive language
- Connecting words with real-world knowledge
- Concept words
- Engaging in print

Modifications for Twos

Introduce fresh or frozen vegetables to the children and give them time to touch, smell, and taste the vegetables. Let them help pour the ingredients into the saucepan. Cook on medium heat and serve.

Expand the Activity

Give each child a piece of white construction paper. With a black marker, draw a large circle on the paper. Cut letters out of different colors of construction paper and place them in a large saucepan. Let the children pick out the letters and glue them onto their "pots" on the construction paper.

BUILD LANGUAGE SKILLS

Vocabulary

- Alphabet
- Soup
- Vegetable
- Corn
- Beans
- Peas
- Pasta
- Stir
- Pan
- Hot
- Mix
- Cook
- Eat

Questions and Things to Say

"Today, we're going to make alphabet soup. We'll make it with chicken broth, pasta, and vegetables. What kind of vegetable is this? That's right—it's corn. Who likes corn? Next, we're going to added peas and beans. Who would like to help me stir the soup?"

Songs, Chants, and Fingerplays

Song: "Alphabet Soup" by Kimberly Bohannon
(Tune: "Hokey Pokey")

We'll put some broth in
And some pasta too.
We'll put some corn in,
Because we're making soup.

We'll stir it in this big pot
Until it's boiling and hot.
That's when we'll eat our soup.

Additional verses: Substitute the ingredients you're adding, such as beans or peas, for the ones in the lyrics.

Be a Friend

MATERIALS

– A poster with three or four classroom rules

Suggested Books

– *Heartprints* by P. K. Hallinan
– *I'm Thankful Each Day!* by P. K. Hallinan
– *Listening Time* by Elizabeth Verdick
– *We Are Best Friends* by Aliki
– *When I Care About Others* by Cornelia Maude Spelman

HOW TO DO IT

Talk to the toddlers about the classroom rules. For example, we are kind to each other, we keep our hands to ourselves, we walk indoors, and we share our toys. The rules should be simple, easy to follow, and posted at eye level in the classroom. Explain why following the rules is important for everyone. Refer to the classroom rules when you are resolving conflict and reinforcing positive behavior in toddlers. In small groups or at circle time, read books or tell stories that teach children how to treat others with respect and how to make friends. Introduce the vocabulary words to the children.

Modifications for Twos

Talk to the children about friendship. Take digital pictures of them treating each other with kindness and respect, and place these around the classroom.

LEARNING OUTCOMES

SOCIAL-EMOTIONAL DEVELOPMENT
* Empathy
* Caring for others
– Sense of self
– Personal identity
– Relationships with adults
– Relationships with peers
– Self-regulation
– Sharing

PHYSICAL DEVELOPMENT
– Perception

COGNITIVE DEVELOPMENT
– Spatial awareness
– Connecting experiences
– Imitating others
– Following simple directions

LANGUAGE DEVELOPMENT
– Receptive language
– Expressive language
– Communicating needs
– Connecting words with real-world knowledge
– Concept words
– Engaging in print
– Using language in play

Expand the Activity

Partner with another teacher in the program and do a friendship exchange. Talk about the friends next door. Teach the children a song, and ask them to sing it to the children in the next room. Ask them to draw pictures for the children about being a friend.

BUILD LANGUAGE SKILLS

Vocabulary

- Friends
- Classroom rules
- Kindness

- Respect
- Hugs
- Sharing

- Being polite
- Nice
- Caring

Questions and Things to Say

"Our classroom rules help us feel safe and show kindness to each other. How do we show our friends kindness? Sharing our toys is a great way to be nice to others. Giving hugs is another way. Thank you for being so kind to each other and sharing your toys so nicely."

Bubblicious

MATERIALS

– Liquid bubble soap
– Large tub or empty sensory table
– Heavy-duty paint aprons or smocks
– Towels
– Water

Suggested Books

– *Bubbles, Bubbles* by Kathi Appelt
– *The Bubble Factory* by Tomie dePaola
– *My Five Senses* by Aliki
– *My Five Senses* by Margaret Miller
– *Pop! A Book About Bubbles*
  by Kimberly Brubaker Bradley

HOW TO DO IT

Place a small amount of liquid bubble soap in the bottom of the tub and fill with water. Swish your hands around to make as many bubbles as possible. Ask the children to watch as you make the bubbles. Show them how you can lift the bubbles up and make mounds and small sculptures. Demonstrate how you can squeeze the bubbles between your fingers. Invite a few children at a time to play and create bubble sculptures. Read the suggested books, introduce the vocabulary words, and sing and chant with the children.

Modifications for Twos

Show the children how to blow on the bubbles and watch how they float in the air.

Expand the Activity

Place toys, such as a rubber duck, baby doll, plastic manipulative, or plastic farm animal, in the water. Let the children experiment with items that float and sink.

LEARNING OUTCOMES

SOCIAL-EMOTIONAL DEVELOPMENT
– Sense of self
– Personal identity
– Relationships with adults
– Relationships with peers
– Self-regulation
– Sharing

PHYSICAL DEVELOPMENT
– Perception
– Fine-motor skills

COGNITIVE DEVELOPMENT
✱ Connecting experiences
✱ Progression of play
– Cause and effect
– Memory
– Spatial awareness
– Imitating others
– Following simple directions

LANGUAGE DEVELOPMENT
– Receptive language
– Expressive language
– Connecting words with real-world knowledge
– Concept words

BUILD LANGUAGE SKILLS

Vocabulary

– Bubbles	– Liquid	– Cold	– Front
– Soft	– Swish	– Tub	– Back
– Wet	– Float	– Squeeze	– Hands
– Water	– Graceful	– Sculptures	– Fingers

Questions and Things to Say

"I'm going to put the liquid bubble soap in the tub. Watch me make bubbles by swishing the water around with my hands. Look how I squeeze the bubbles with my hands. Can you join me? What do you feel? I feel the soft bubbles. Do your hands feel wet? What sculptures can you make out of the bubbles?"

Songs, Chants, and Fingerplays

Song: "Pop Goes the Bubble" by Kimberly Bohannon
(Tune: "Pop! Goes the Weasel")

All around us bubbles float.
They're moving soft and graceful.
All around us bubbles float.
(Pop a bubble with your finger)
Pop goes the bubble.

Bugs and Insects

MATERIALS

– Books and photographs of bugs
– Insects
– Toy bugs

Suggested Books

– *Are You a Butterfly?* by Judy Allen
  and Tudor Humphries
– *Are You a Ladybug?* by Judy Allen
  and Tudor Humphries
– *Bugs! Bugs! Bugs!* by Bob Barner

HOW TO DO IT

Show the children photographs of bugs and
insects, such as spiders, bees, ladybugs, beetles,
butterflies, and fireflies. Name each bug and insect,
and point out their unique features, patterns, and
colors. In a small group, let the children look at
the toy bugs and insects and pass them to their
neighbor. Read the suggested books, introduce the
vocabulary words, and sing and chant with the
children.

Modifications for Twos

Explain in more detail about bugs and insects. Go for a nature walk and point out what you
see outdoors. Afterward, ask the children to draw what they saw. Write their descriptions of
the bugs or insects on the backs of their drawings.

Expand the Activity

Cut out twelve to fifteen ants about 3 to 4 inches wide from black construction paper.
Weave a trail of ants around the classroom. Ask the children to walk around the ants to
the sound of marching music. Talk about the importance of caring for nature and the
environment.

LEARNING OUTCOMES

SOCIAL-EMOTIONAL DEVELOPMENT
✱ Caring for others
– Sense of self
– Relationships with adults
– Relationships with peers
– Empathy
– Sharing

PHYSICAL DEVELOPMENT
– Perception
– Fine-motor skills

COGNITIVE DEVELOPMENT
– Memory
– Spatial awareness
– Connecting experiences
– Number awareness
– Following simple directions

LANGUAGE DEVELOPMENT
✱ Connecting words with
  real-world knowledge
– Receptive language
– Expressive language
– Concept words
– Engaging in print

BUILD LANGUAGE SKILLS

Vocabulary

- Bugs
- Insects
- Spiders
- Bees
- Ladybugs
- Beetles
- Butterflies
- Fireflies
- Fly
- Crawl
- Hop

Questions and Things to Say

"There are many different bugs and insects. Here's a picture of a ladybug. What do we see? It's red with tiny black spots. It lives on plants, and it flies. Watch as it crawls on my arm. Would you like to have it crawl on your arm too?"

Songs, Chants, and Fingerplays

Song: "Bees, Beetles, Bugs" by Jean Barbre (Tune: "Three Blind Mice")

Bees, beetles, bugs.
Bees, beetles, bugs.
See how they hop.
See how they hop.
They hop on top of the green, green leaves.
They hop on top of the green, green leaves.
Bees, beetles, bugs.

Bees, beetles, bugs.
Bees, beetles, bugs.
See how they fly.
See how they fly.
They fly in the sky as we watch them go by.
They fly in the sky as we watch them go by.
Bees, beetles, bugs.

Song: "Baby Bumblebee" (traditional)

Dump and Fill

MATERIALS

– Large and small unbreakable containers
– An assortment of items for filling and dumping containers (such as large beads, toy farm animals, ABC blocks, and large pegs)

Suggested Books

– *Colors, ABC, Numbers* by Roger Priddy
– *Dig Dig Digging* by Margaret Mayo
– *Richard Scarry's Best First Book Ever!* by Richard Scarry

HOW TO DO IT

Toddlers love to fill containers with items and then dump them out. Place all of the items in the large containers and invite the children to dump them out. You need to demonstrate how to fill the containers so they can be dumped again. Talk to the children about how many items they can get in a container and how the items sound when they are dumped out. Read the suggested books, introduce the vocabulary words, and sing and chant with the children.

Modifications for Twos

Add sand to large containers and repeat the activity. Do this outside or at a sand table.

Expand the Activity

Ask the children to sort and count the items with you. Demonstrate how to stack smaller containers into a larger one. This will help children learn to clean up and put things where they belong.

LEARNING OUTCOMES

SOCIAL-EMOTIONAL DEVELOPMENT
– Sense of self
– Personal identity
– Relationships with adults
– Relationships with peers
– Sharing

PHYSICAL DEVELOPMENT
– Perception
– Fine-motor skills

COGNITIVE DEVELOPMENT
✷ Cause and effect
✷ Connecting experiences
– Memory
– Spatial awareness
– Number awareness
– Imitating others
– Progression of play
– Following simple directions

LANGUAGE DEVELOPMENT
– Receptive language
– Expressive language
– Communicating needs
– Connecting words with real-world knowledge
– Concept words
– Using language in play

BUILD LANGUAGE SKILLS

Vocabulary

- Fill
- Dump
- Pour
- Top
- Empty
- Feel
- Count
- Measuring cups
- Plastic containers

Questions and Things to Say

"Help me dump all the toys into this large container. Watch while I fill the smaller container with the toys. Listen to the sound it makes when I dump them out. What does it sound like? Here's a container for you. What do you want to put in your container to dump?"

Songs, Chants, and Fingerplays

Song: "Fill and Dump" by Kimberly Bohannon
(Tune: "Row, Row, Row Your Boat")

Fill, fill, fill it up,	Dump, dump, dump it out,
Fill it to the top,	Dump it into here,
Fill it 'til it's nice and full,	Dump until there's nothing left,
And then it's time to stop.	What sound do you hear?

Egg-a-Cracken

MATERIALS

– Clean dry eggshells* from three dozen eggs
– Construction paper
– Food coloring
– Water
– Slotted spoon for dipping
– Small bowls
– Paper towels
– Glue

*To make empty eggshells, poke a small hole in both ends of a raw egg and empty the egg into a small bowl or container. Refrigerate the raw egg to use later for cooking. Rinse the eggshells with water and let them air-dry overnight.

Suggested Books

– *Dora's Eggs* by Julia Sykes
– *First the Egg* by Laura Vaccaro Seeger
– *My Five Senses* by Aliki
– *My Five Senses* by Margaret Miller
– *National Geographic Little Kids First Big Book of Animals* by Catherine D. Hughes

LEARNING OUTCOMES

SOCIAL–EMOTIONAL DEVELOPMENT
– Relationships with adults
– Relationships with peers
– Caring for others
– Sharing

PHYSICAL DEVELOPMENT
✶ Perception
✶ Fine-motor skills

COGNITIVE DEVELOPMENT
– Cause and effect
– Memory
– Spatial awareness
– Connecting experiences
– Imitating others
– Following simple directions

LANGUAGE DEVELOPMENT
– Receptive language
– Expressive language
– Communicating needs
– Connecting words with real-world knowledge
– Concept words
– Using language in play

HOW TO DO IT

Note: Make sure none of the children are allergic to eggs first.

Give each child a piece of construction paper. Let them watch while you dip the eggshells into the water tinted with food coloring. Talk about the different colors as the eggshells change colors. Let the eggshells dry on the paper towels. Demonstrate how to crack them, and let the children try. Once all the different-colored eggshells are cracked, let the children glue the pieces on construction paper. Talk about the shapes and designs they are making. Read the suggested books, introduce the vocabulary words, and sing and chant with the children.

Modifications for Twos

With supervision, two-year-olds can tint and crack the eggshells themselves. Place the eggshells in a plastic bag. Use a large wooden spoon to crack them.

Expand the Activity

Show children books about animals that lay eggs, such as *National Geographic Little Kids First Big Book of Animals*. Hard-boil and cool several eggs. Let the children feel one of them. Cut it in half and describe the yolk and white. Ask the children what they see, feel, and smell. Use the remaining hard-boiled eggs as part of their snack.

BUILD LANGUAGE SKILLS

Vocabulary

- Eggs
- Eggshells
- Tint
- Glue
- Crack
- Crunch
- Design
- Rough
- Smooth
- Plain
- Colored
- Smell

Questions and Things to Say

"Lots of animals lay eggs. Let's look and feel the eggshell. Does it feel smooth or rough? Watch while we dip it in the colored water. What color is it now? Listen when we crack the eggs. Do you hear the crunch?"

Songs, Chants, and Fingerplays

Chant: "Humpty Dumpty" (traditional)

Fishing with My Friends

MATERIALS

- Several 3-foot wooden dowels
- Medium-heavy cording cut 2 to 3 feet long
- Metal washers (commonly found at hardware stores)
- Electrical tape
- Magnetic letters
- Magnetic numbers

Note: You can purchase a children's magnetic fishing set at a toy store instead of making one.

Suggested Books

- *Colors, ABC, Numbers* by Roger Priddy
- *Where Is My Friend?* by Simms Taback

HOW TO DO IT

To make the fishing poles, tie a metal washer to the end of a length of cord. Attach the cord to the end of a wooden dowel using electrical tape. Place the magnetic items for fishing in an empty water or sensory table. Demonstrate how the washer sticks to the magnetic items. Let the children pull the letters and numbers out of the water. Place the magnetic items back in the sensory table to be used again. Read the suggested books, introduce the vocabulary words, and sing and chant with the children.

Modifications for Twos

Identify the letters and numbers as the children pull them up. Cut out small pictures of fish, and adhere them to card stock. Place a small piece of magnetic tape on the back so children can continue fishing.

LEARNING OUTCOMES

SOCIAL-EMOTIONAL DEVELOPMENT
- ✱ Relationships with peers
- ✱ Self-regulation
- Sense of self
- Relationships with adults
- Caring for others
- Sharing

PHYSICAL DEVELOPMENT
- Fine-motor skills

COGNITIVE DEVELOPMENT
- Cause and effect
- Memory
- Spatial awareness
- Connecting experiences
- Number awareness
- Imitating others
- Progression of play
- Following simple directions

LANGUAGE DEVELOPMENT
- Receptive language
- Expressive language
- Connecting words with real-world knowledge
- Concept words
- Using language in play

Expand the Activity

Repeat this activity placing the waterproof items in a sensory table filled with water or sand.

BUILD LANGUAGE SKILLS

Vocabulary

- Fishing pond
- Magnetic letters
- Magnetic numbers
- Pull
- Catch
- Fish
- Drop
- Sink
- Float

Questions and Things to Say

"We're going to drop our fishing lines over the edge and see if we can catch a letter or number. The magnet will help us pull it up. There you go! You got the letter *C*. Pull the letter off the magnet and drop it back in the water."

Songs, Chants, and Fingerplays

Song: "Fishing with My Friends" by Jean Barbre
(Tune: "The Farmer in the Dell")

I'm fishing with my friends,
Fishing with my friends,
Hi-ho! The letters go!
I'm fishing with my friends.

I caught an *A*.
I caught an *A*.
Hi-ho! The letters go!
I caught an *A*.

Additional verses:
You can substitute other letters
of the alphabet, or numbers.

Fun with Fingerpainting

MATERIALS

– Butcher paper
– Ingredients and tools for making fingerpaint:
  › Large bowl or heavy saucepan
  › Large metal spoon
  › Flour or cornstarch
  › Water
  › Food coloring
  › Measuring cups
  › Small bowls

Suggested Books

– *Blue Hat, Green Hat* by Sandra Boynton
– *My Five Senses* by Aliki
– *My Five Senses* by Margaret Miller
– *Rosie's Walk* by Pat Hutchins
– *White Rabbit's Color Book* by Alan Baker

HOW TO DO IT

Place butcher paper on the floor or table. Place small amounts of fingerpaint in front of the children and let them begin painting. Here are two simple fingerpaint recipes:

Recipe one:
mix 2 cups white flour, 2 cups cold water, and food coloring in a large bowl. Stir until lumps are gone.

Recipe two:
mix ½ cup cornstarch and 2 cups cold water in a heavy saucepan. Stir until lumps are gone. Cook, stirring constantly, until mixture is thick. It will boil. Pour into small bowls and add food coloring. Let cool before using.

This activity is also fun for children to do outdoors on a sunny day. Be sure they wash their hands before and after participating. Read the suggested books and introduce the vocabulary words to the children.

LEARNING OUTCOMES

SOCIAL-EMOTIONAL DEVELOPMENT
– Sense of self
– Personal identity
– Relationships with adults
– Sharing

PHYSICAL DEVELOPMENT
– Perception
– Fine-motor skills

COGNITIVE DEVELOPMENT
✱ Progression of play
– Cause and effect
– Memory
– Spatial awareness
– Connecting experiences

LANGUAGE DEVELOPMENT
✱ Concept words
– Receptive language
– Expressive language
– Connecting words with real-world knowledge

Modifications for Twos

Make edible fingerpaint by mixing one package of vanilla instant pudding according to the directions. Place small amounts of the pudding into individual bowls and add food coloring for different colors. Invite the children to fingerpaint and explain that this time they can lick their fingers!

Expand the Activity

Let children paint with plastic spoons, washable farm or jungle animals, sponges, or feathers to experiment more with paint.

BUILD LANGUAGE SKILLS

Vocabulary

- Paint
- Wet
- Colors
- Fingers
- Sticky
- Paper
- Cold
- Messy
- Dry

Questions and Things to Say

"Who would like to fingerpaint today? I have three colors to choose from—red, yellow, and blue. What color would you like to use? How does the paint feel? Does it feel sticky?"

Get the Wiggles Out

MATERIALS

– Any music with lots of rhythm (such as Greg and Steve's *Kids in Motion, Jumpin' and Jammin'*, or *Shake, Rattle, and Rock*)

Suggested Books

– *Barnyard Dance!* by Sandra Boynton
– *Dancing Feet!* by Lindsey Craig
– *Hippos Go Berserk!* by Sandra Boynton

HOW TO DO IT

On rainy days, when children can't go outside, or when there is a lot of energy in the classroom, gather the children together and pick a song to play. You can model getting the wiggles out by moving your body around. Make sure there's lots of room so children can move without running into each other. After playing the fast songs, select a slower-paced one while you move to another activity. Read the suggested books, introduce the vocabulary words, and sing and chant with the children.

Modifications for Twos

Let the children decide which of their favorite songs to play. Play the music and let them dance and wiggle. At the end, ask them to move from wiggling into quiet positions.

Expand the Activity

Encourage children to use scarves or musical instruments while they listen and move to the music.

LEARNING OUTCOMES

SOCIAL-EMOTIONAL DEVELOPMENT
* Self-regulation
– Sense of self
– Relationships with adults
– Relationships with peers

PHYSICAL DEVELOPMENT
– Gross-motor skills

COGNITIVE DEVELOPMENT
– Spatial awareness
– Connecting experiences
– Imitating others
– Progression of play
– Following simple directions

LANGUAGE DEVELOPMENT
* Engaging in music, rhythm, and rhyme
– Receptive language
– Expressive language
– Concept words

BUILD LANGUAGE SKILLS

Vocabulary

- Music
- Energy
- Start
- Stop
- Jump
- Hop
- Wiggle
- Move
- Swing

Questions and Things to Say

"We can't go outside today because it's raining. Instead, we're going to listen to a song and get all our wiggles out. Can you wiggle your body for me? Good. Be careful not to run into each other. Let's wiggle and dance!"

Songs, Chants, and Fingerplays

Song: "I've Got Wiggles" by Kimberly Bohannon
(Tune: "If You're Happy and You Know It")

I've got wiggles, wiggles, wiggles inside me.
I've got wiggles, wiggles, wiggles inside me.
I've got wiggles, wiggles, wiggles.
I've got wiggles, wiggles, wiggles.
I've got wiggles, wiggles, wiggles inside me.

Chant: "I Wiggle" (traditional)

I'm Glad I'm Me

MATERIALS

Suggested Books

- *ABC I Like Me!* by Nancy Carlson
- *Today I Feel Silly: And Other Moods That Make My Day* by Jamie Lee Curtis
- *We Are All Alike—We Are All Different* by Cheltenham Elementary School Kindergartners

HOW TO DO IT

Describe how each child is alike and different from their peers. Talk about differences and similarities, such as eye and hair colors. Emphasize how everyone is a special and unique individual. Ask children what they like to do at home and what they like to play with at school. Read the suggested books and introduce the vocabulary words to the children.

Modifications for Twos

Let older children draw a picture of themselves. On the back of the paper, write the child's description of what makes him feel special and unique.

Expand the Activity

In a small group, encourage the children to share one or two things they like about themselves, such as playing outdoors or painting. You may want to have the children hold up photographs of themselves during their turn.

LEARNING OUTCOMES

SOCIAL-EMOTIONAL DEVELOPMENT
- ✱ Personal identity
- ✱ Empathy
- – Sense of self
- – Relationships with adults
- – Relationships with peers
- – Caring for others
- – Sharing

PHYSICAL DEVELOPMENT
- – Perception
- – Gross-motor skills
- – Fine-motor skills

COGNITIVE DEVELOPMENT
- – Memory
- – Spatial awareness
- – Connecting experiences
- – Imitating others

LANGUAGE DEVELOPMENT
- – Receptive language
- – Expressive language
- – Connecting words with real-world knowledge
- – Concept words

BUILD LANGUAGE SKILLS

Vocabulary

- Eyes
- Green
- Blue
- Brown

- Black
- Blond
- Hair
- Smile

- Curly
- Straight
- Wavy
- Similar

- Alike
- Different
- Special
- Unique

Questions and Things to Say

"We're all people, and each of us is unique and special. We need to treat each other with kindness and respect. We all have hair on our heads. Let's touch our heads and feel our hair. Some of us have straight hair and others have curly hair. Let's see who has curly hair? Who has straight hair? I'm going to pass around the mirror so you can look and see what kind of hair you have."

I'm Puzzled!

MATERIALS

– Puzzles representing colors, shapes, numbers, and objects such as cars, trucks, and people
– Wooden puzzles with four to six pieces for young children

Suggested Books

– *Colors, ABC, Numbers* by Roger Priddy
– *My Big Animal Book* by Roger Priddy
– *Richard Scarry's Best First Book Ever!* by Richard Scarry

HOW TO DO IT

Select a puzzle that you and the child can work on together. Talk about the puzzle before you take out the pieces. Let the child dump the pieces on the floor. Discuss the feel of the pieces, and talk about their tops and bottoms and the color and texture of the wood. Model how to put the puzzle together. Guide the child as she learns to put the puzzle together. If a puzzle doesn't have big knobs on it, you can glue kitchen knobs to each piece. Read the suggested books and introduce the vocabulary words to the children.

Modifications for Twos

Introduce puzzles with images of children playing or showing emotions. Help the children build their vocabularies with the puzzle pictures.

Expand the Activity

Introduce puzzles that have more pieces and tell a story or talk about an event, such as children playing at the beach. Talk about the picture, and ask children questions about the picture.

LEARNING OUTCOMES

SOCIAL-EMOTIONAL DEVELOPMENT
– Sense of self
– Personal identity
– Relationships with adults
– Sharing

PHYSICAL DEVELOPMENT
– Perception
– Fine-motor skills

COGNITIVE DEVELOPMENT
✱ Memory
– Cause and effect
– Spatial awareness
– Connecting experiences
– Number awareness
– Imitating others
– Progression of play
– Following simple directions

LANGUAGE DEVELOPMENT
✱ Receptive language
– Expressive language
– Communicating needs
– Connecting words with real-world knowledge
– Concept words
– Using language in play

BUILD LANGUAGE SKILLS

Vocabulary

- Puzzle
- Pieces
- Wood

- Put
- Place
- Move

- Edge
- Smooth
- Rough

- Top
- Bottom

Questions and Things to Say

"This puzzle shows pictures of five birds. I'm going to point at and count them: one, two, three, four, and five. Here is the red bird, the blue bird, the yellow bird, the green bird, and the purple bird. Point to them with me. Where do you think the red bird goes? Can you put the red bird in the puzzle?"

77

Jars of Music

MATERIALS

- Five or six glass jars of different sizes and shapes
- Water
- Pitcher
- A wooden spoon
- A metal spoon

Suggested Books

- *Gray Rabbit's Odd One Out* by Alan Baker
- *My Five Senses* by Aliki
- *My Five Senses* by Margaret Miller
- *Opposites* by Sandra Boynton
- *Rosie's Walk* by Pat Hutchins

HOW TO DO IT

Fill a pitcher with water and pour it into different-size glass jars, varying the amount of water in each jar. Demonstrate how each jar sounds different when you tap on the glass. Tap the jars with the wooden and metal spoons at the top and bottom, and talk about the different sounds you hear. Read the suggested books, introduce the vocabulary words, and sing and chant with the children.

Modifications for Twos

Let older children pour the water into the jars themselves. They can add food coloring to the jars. Talk about the colors of the water.

Expand the Activity

Select two identical short jars and one tall, narrow jar. Fill the short jars with the same amount of water, and ask the children to listen to the sound the jars make when tapped. Say that the jars have the same amount of water. Pour the water from one of the short jars into the tall, narrow jar. Talk about how the jars look different but contain the same amount of water.

LEARNING OUTCOMES

SOCIAL-EMOTIONAL DEVELOPMENT
- Sense of self
- Relationships with adults
- Relationships with peers
- Sharing

PHYSICAL DEVELOPMENT
✱ Perception
- Fine-motor skills

COGNITIVE DEVELOPMENT
✱ Spatial awareness
- Cause and effect
- Memory
- Connecting experiences
- Imitating others
- Following simple directions

LANGUAGE DEVELOPMENT
- Receptive language
- Expressive language
- Connecting words with real-world knowledge
- Concept words
- Using language in play

BUILD LANGUAGE SKILLS

Vocabulary

– Jars	– There	– Fill	– Tall
– Tap	– Top	– Space	– Small
– Lower	– Bottom	– Sound	– Narrow
– Higher	– Wooden spoon	– More	
– Here	– Metal spoon	– Less	

Questions and Things to Say

"We're going to fill the jars with water. Which jar has more water in it? Does it sound different when we tap the top of the glass rather than the bottom? Listen carefully. Which jar sounds lower? Which jar sounds higher? How does the metal spoon sound when we tap it against the jars?"

Songs, Chants, and Fingerplays

Song: "Tap, Tap, Tap" by Jean Barbre
(Tune: "Row, Row, Row Your Boat")

Tap, tap, tap the jar,
Listen to the sound.
Tap the jar, tap the jar,
There's music all around.
Here, hear, hear the noise,
Listen to the sound.
Tap it here, tap it there,
There's music all around.

78

Little Helpers

MATERIALS

Suggested Books

- *Friends at School* by Rochelle Bunnett
- *Richard Scarry's Please and Thank You Book* by Richard Scarry
- *A Splendid Friend, Indeed* by Suzanne Bloom

HOW TO DO IT

Young children love to help. Plan activities that help them learn to help and care for others. Throughout the day, encourage them to help—for example, by passing items like cups, napkins, or snacks. Recognize and identify helping behavior. Children will make mistakes while they're learning. Try not to correct them or redo their efforts. Perfection is not important here; focus on their acts of helping. Read the suggested books, introduce the vocabulary words, and sing and chant with the children.

Modifications for Twos

Encourage children to say "please" and "thank you" to their peers when they're helping. Talk about manners, and model polite language.

Expand the Activity

Each day, select children to be the special helpers of the day. Place their names on the helper list. Helpers can do a variety of things—for example, pass out snacks, give each child a crayon or a piece of paper for an art activity, carry items for outdoor play, or pick a song to sing.

LEARNING OUTCOMES

SOCIAL-EMOTIONAL DEVELOPMENT
✱ Caring for others
✱ Sharing
- Sense of self
- Personal identity
- Relationships with adults
- Relationships with peers
- Self-regulation
- Empathy

PHYSICAL DEVELOPMENT
- Fine-motor skills

COGNITIVE DEVELOPMENT
- Cause and effect
- Memory
- Connecting experiences
- Imitating others
- Following simple directions

LANGUAGE DEVELOPMENT
- Receptive language
- Expressive language
- Communicating needs
- Connecting words with real-world knowledge
- Concept words

BUILD LANGUAGE SKILLS

Vocabulary

- Please
- Thank you
- Share

- Pass
- Help
- Helper

- Friends
- Caring
- Clean up

Questions and Things to Say

"It's important to help and care for each other. Helping other people is a nice thing to do. Who wants to help me pass out our snack today? Let's thank Carlos for helping us with snack."

Songs, Chants, and Fingerplays

Song: "Thank You to Our Friends" by Kimberly Bohannon
(Tune: "Frère Jacques")

Thank you, thank you.
Thank you, thank you.
You're so kind, you're so kind.
Thanks so much for helping.
Thanks so much for helping.
You're my friend, you're my friend.

Making Space for Stripes

MATERIALS

– Objects with stripes and patterns (such as toy zebras, frogs, fish, leaves, a United States flag, or photographs with stripes and patterns)

Suggested Books

– *Biggest, Strongest, Fastest* by Steve Jenkins
– *Lots and Lots of Zebra Stripes: Patterns in Nature* by Stephen R. Swinburne

HOW TO DO IT

Show children objects and photographs of things with stripes and patterns. Point out which children are wearing stripes or patterns, such as plaids or checks. Ask the children to find more stripes and patterns in the room. Read the suggested books, introduce the vocabulary words, and sing and chant with the children.

LEARNING OUTCOMES

SOCIAL-EMOTIONAL DEVELOPMENT
– Personal identity
– Relationships with adults
– Relationships with peers

PHYSICAL DEVELOPMENT
– Perception

COGNITIVE DEVELOPMENT
✶ Number awareness
– Memory
– Spatial awareness
– Connecting experiences

LANGUAGE DEVELOPMENT
✶ Expressive language
– Receptive language
– Connecting words with real-world knowledge
– Concept words
– Engaging in print

Modifications for Twos

Help the children look for stripes and patterns indoors and outdoors. Point out the patterns in the floor, windowpanes, and on outdoor benches. Draw stripes or patterns on chart paper or on the sidewalk.

Expand the Activity

Cut strips of colored construction paper and ask the children to glue them onto white paper to create patterns and stripes. Introduce to the children a simple A-B pattern.

BUILD LANGUAGE SKILLS

Vocabulary

- Stripes
- Patterns
- Checks
- Floor
- Window
- Door
- Line
- Straight

Questions and Things to Say

"Here's a toy zebra. The zebra has stripes on his coat. A stripe is a long narrow strip against a plain background. Look at your own clothes and see if you're wearing stripes. Who has stripes on their shirts? What colors are the stripes? What else do you see with stripes?"

Songs, Chants, and Fingerplays

Chant: "Stripes Are Everywhere" by Kimberly Bohannon

Stripes are everywhere.
We see them here and there.
Long and short,
Thick and thin,
Let's go look and find them.

Chant: "Five Little Speckled Frogs" (traditional)

March to the Drum

MATERIALS

- Marching music
- A variety of musical instruments

Suggested Books

- *Bats on Parade* by Kathi Appelt
- *Curious George at the Parade* by Margret Rey and H. A. Rey
- *Dino Parade* by Thom Wiley

HOW TO DO IT

Show the children how to march. Explain that marching is different from walking. Invite the children to practice marching in place. Let children pick out a musical instrument or a homemade drum (see Tom-Tom Drum, activity 98). Play marching music and encourage children to practice marching. Read the suggested books, introduce the vocabulary words, and sing and chant with the children.

Modifications for Twos

Ask children to form a line and march around the room or march to a nearby classroom as if they're on parade. Encourage them to play their instruments as they march around.

Expand the Activity

Older children can practice marching slowly and raising their knees high. Give them hats to wear while they march and play their musical instruments.

LEARNING OUTCOMES

SOCIAL-EMOTIONAL DEVELOPMENT
- ★ Relationships with peers
- – Sense of self
- – Personal identity
- – Relationships with adults
- – Self-regulation
- – Sharing

PHYSICAL DEVELOPMENT
- – Perception
- – Gross-motor skills
- – Fine-motor skills

COGNITIVE DEVELOPMENT
- ★ Following simple directions
- – Cause and effect
- – Memory
- – Spatial awareness
- – Connecting experiences
- – Imitating others
- – Progression of play

LANGUAGE DEVELOPMENT
- – Receptive language
- – Expressive language
- – Connecting words with real-world knowledge
- – Concept words
- – Engaging in music, rhythm, and rhyme
- – Using language in play

BUILD LANGUAGE SKILLS

Vocabulary

- March
- Marching music
- Play
- Tap
- Instruments
- Tom-tom drum
- Knees
- Slowly
- High
- Stop

Questions and Things to Say

"Marching is like walking, but it's different. When we march, we lift our knees high. Watch me as I march. Let's all try."

Songs, Chants, and Fingerplays

Song: "Make a Sound" by Jean Barbre
(Tune: "This Old Man")

Make a sound,
Make a sound.
Play your instruments nice and loud.
Play them fast, play them slow,
Play it any way you know.
Now play your instruments. Here we go!
Tap your drum,
Tap your drum.
Tap your drum with a rum-tum-tum,
Hit it high, hit it low,
Play it any way you know.
Now play your instruments. Here we go!

Chant: "Marching Beat"
by Kimberly Bohannon

Keep the rhythm,
Yes, keep the beat,
March around
And move your feet.
Keep the rhythm,
Yes, keep the beat,
Play your drum
And move your feet.

My Pets

MATERIALS

– Photographs of animals a family might have as pets (such as dogs, cats, birds, and hamsters)

Suggested Books

– *Doggies: A Counting and Barking Book* by Sandra Boynton
– *Dogs and Cats* by Steve Jenkins
– *Dot the Fire Dog* by Lisa Desimini
– *Harry the Dirty Dog* by Gene Zion
– *Whose Nose?* by Jeannette Rowe

HOW TO DO IT

Show the children photographs of animals. Talk with them about different animals, including the animal's tail, ears, whiskers, and fur. Discuss what the animals eat, how they communicate, where they sleep, and how we care for them as pets. Invite children to share photographs of their pets and tell something about them. Share the importance of being gentle with animals. Read the suggested books, introduce the vocabulary words, and sing and chant with the children.

Modifications for Twos

Talk to children about what their pets do and why they like them. Let children paint, using animal-shaped stamps and cookie cutters. Talk about the different shapes, such as paws, bones, cats, and dogs.

Expand the Activity

Turn the dramatic play area into a veterinarian office. Place a play stethoscope, bandages, clipboard, pencil, stuffed animals, and large white shirt in the area. Write "Dr. Bones's Veterinarian Hospital" on a sign in the area.

LEARNING OUTCOMES

SOCIAL-EMOTIONAL DEVELOPMENT
* Caring for others
– Personal identity
– Relationships with adults
– Empathy
– Sharing

PHYSICAL DEVELOPMENT
– Perception
– Fine-motor skills

COGNITIVE DEVELOPMENT
– Memory
– Connecting experiences

LANGUAGE DEVELOPMENT
* Communicating needs
– Receptive language
– Expressive language
– Connecting words with real-world knowledge
– Concept words
– Engaging in print

BUILD LANGUAGE SKILLS

Vocabulary

- Touch
- Gentle
- Love
- Care

- Friends
- Respect
- Dogs
- Cats

- Bunny
- Fish
- Hamster
- Fur

- Coats
- Whiskers
- Tongues
- Tail

Questions and Things to Say

"How many of you have pets at home? Who can tell us the name of their pets? What do you like best about your dog, Buster? Where does he sleep? What does he eat? Do you help take care of him?"

Songs, Chants, and Fingerplays

Song: "This Old Man" (traditional)
Song: "Bingo" (traditional)
Song: "Six Little Ducks" (traditional)
Chant: "Three Little Kittens" (traditional)

Orange Peel

MATERIALS

– Fresh oranges
– Cutting board
– Paper napkins

Suggested Books

– *Mouse's First Day of School* by Lauren Thompson
– *My Five Senses* by Aliki
– *My Five Senses* by Margaret Miller
– *White Rabbit's Color Book* by Alan Baker

HOW TO DO IT

Let the children feel and smell the oranges before you peel them. Talk about the round shape of the oranges, the bumpy surface, the navel, and the orange color. Be sure to wash each orange before you peel and serve it. Begin to slowly peel the orange and describe what you are doing. Describe the inner flesh and juicy portion of the fruit. Pass the peel around for the children to feel and smell. Serve pieces of the fruit as a snack. Read the suggested books, introduce the vocabulary words, and sing and chant with the children.

Modifications for Twos

Let older children look at the outside and inside of the orange peel with a magnifying glass. Talk about the peel and how it feels. If the oranges have seeds, describe the seeds and let older children feel them. Juice the oranges and talk about the pulp.

Expand the Activity

Leave the peel in the sunshine. Let the children examine what happens when the peel dries and the edges curl. You can also help children identify objects in the room that are the color orange.

LEARNING OUTCOMES

SOCIAL-EMOTIONAL DEVELOPMENT
– Relationships with adults
– Relationships with peers
– Sharing

PHYSICAL DEVELOPMENT
✱ Perception
– Fine-motor skills

COGNITIVE DEVELOPMENT
– Memory
– Spatial awareness
– Connecting experiences

LANGUAGE DEVELOPMENT
✱ Connecting words with real-world knowledge
– Receptive language
– Expressive language
– Concept words

BUILD LANGUAGE SKILLS

Vocabulary

- Orange
- Peel
- Seeds
- Navel

- Juice
- Sweet
- Pulp
- Bumpy

- Thick
- Thin
- Round
- Fresh

- Fruit

Questions and Things to Say

"Oranges are fruit, and they are round. Oranges are the color orange. How does the orange feel, smell, and taste? Is the peel bumpy? Is it sweet?"

Songs, Chants, and Fingerplays

Song: "Orange Orange" by Jean Barbre
(Tune: "Frère Jacques")

Orange, orange.
Orange, orange.
I like you.
I like you.
You are sweet and juicy.
You are sweet and juicy.
Juice and pulp.
Juice and pulp.

Over the Moon for You

MATERIALS

– Photographs of the moon and stars

Suggested Books

– *Bear Snores On* by Karma Wilson
– *Goodnight Moon* by Margaret Wise Brown
– *Harold and the Purple Crayon*
  by Crockett Johnson
– *Mommy's Little Star* by Janet Bingham
– *On the Seashore* by Anna Milborne

HOW TO DO IT

Share facts about the sun and moon with the children. Show them photographs of the moon and stars. Demonstrate how to draw stars with five points. Count the points of the star. Read any of the suggested books, and ask the children to point to the moon and stars on the pages. Ask families to show the children the moon and stars at night. Read the suggested books, introduce the vocabulary words, and sing and chant with the children.

LEARNING OUTCOMES

SOCIAL-EMOTIONAL DEVELOPMENT
– Relationships with adults
– Relationships with peers
– Caring for others

PHYSICAL DEVELOPMENT
– Perception
– Fine-motor skills

COGNITIVE DEVELOPMENT
✶ Memory
✶ Number awareness
– Spatial awareness
– Connecting experiences
– Progression of play
– Following simple directions

LANGUAGE DEVELOPMENT
– Receptive language
– Expressive language
– Concept words
– Engaging in print
– Engaging in music, rhythm, and rhyme

Modifications for Twos

Cut circles, squares, diamonds, rectangles, and stars from construction paper. Help the children sort and count the different shapes. Read the story *On the Seashore* and show the children the picture of the hermit crab and the three starfish. Talk with the children about the starfish in the ocean and the stars in the sky.

Expand the Activity

Cut 4- to 5-inch stars and moons out of tagboard. Provide children with paint, and let them paint with star-shaped stamps and cookie cutters. Sprinkle the shapes with glitter for extra sparkle. Punch a hole in the tagboard, and hang their stars and moons from the ceiling with fishing line or string.

BUILD LANGUAGE SKILLS

Vocabulary

- Star
- Moon
- Twinkle
- Light
- Shine
- Points

- Sky
- Stamps
- Cookie cutters
- Shapes
- Circle
- Square

- Diamond
- Rectangle
- Hermit crab
- Shells
- Starfish

Questions and Things to Say

"This is the shape of a star. It has five points. Count the points with me: one, two, three, four, and five. At night, we can see the stars because the sun isn't shining. The moon is bright at night too. I'm going to read you the book *Mommy's Little Star.* Can you see the moon and stars on the cover of the book?"

Songs, Chants, and Fingerplays

Song: "The Moon and Stars" by Jean Barbre
(Tune: "My Bonnie Lies over the Ocean")

The moon lies over the meadows.
The moon lies over the sea.
The moon lies over the mountains.
And lights up the nighttime for me.

Song: "Twinkle, Twinkle, Little Star" (traditional)

Chant: "Hey, Diddle, Diddle!" (traditional)

Chant: "Starlight, Star Bright" (traditional)

Paper Bag Baby

MATERIALS

- Different kinds of paper (such as paper towels, wax paper, tissue paper, wrapping paper with a pattern or design, contact paper, sandpaper, flocked paper, newspaper, construction paper, and magazine paper)
- Scissors
- Glue
- Plastic sheet protectors
- Labels
- Marker
- Half-inch three-ring binder

Suggested Books

- *Baby Touch and Feel Animals* by DK Publishing
- *My Five Senses* by Aliki
- *My Five Senses* by Margaret Miller
- *What Can You Do with a Paper Bag?* by Judith Cressy

LEARNING OUTCOMES

SOCIAL-EMOTIONAL DEVELOPMENT
- Personal identity
- Relationships with adults
- Relationships with peers
- Sharing

PHYSICAL DEVELOPMENT
- Perception
- Fine-motor skills

COGNITIVE DEVELOPMENT
- Memory
- Spatial awareness
- Number awareness
- Following simple directions

LANGUAGE DEVELOPMENT
* Connecting words with real-world knowledge
- Concept words
- Receptive language
- Expressive language
- Engaging in print
- Using language in play

HOW TO DO IT

Cut the different types of paper into 5-inch squares and glue them to individual sheets of 8.5-by-11-inch construction paper. Sit on the floor with the children and introduce them to the different kinds of paper. Let them explore the paper. Ask them to pass it to their neighbor. When they are finished, place each piece of paper in a plastic sheet protector, label it, and put the sheets in a half-inch binder. Place the binder where the children can easily reach it. Show them the pictures from the book *What Can You Do with a Paper Bag?* Read the other suggested books, introduce the vocabulary words, and sing and chant with the children.

Modifications for Twos

Cut 2-by-4-inch pieces of each kind of paper and glue the pieces to 3-by-5-inch index cards. Label the cards with the name of the paper. Demonstrate how to match the paper squares to the larger pieces of paper. Place the index cards in a paper bag. Ask the children to take turns pulling out a card and matching it to the corresponding piece of paper.

Expand the Activity

Encourage children to make a paper collage by gluing small pieces of paper to construction paper. Provide them with different types and colors of paper. You can also show them how to crumble colored tissue paper and glue it to the collage to add a 3-D effect. Children can also glue fabric, yarn, feathers, and small pieces of ribbon to their artwork.

BUILD LANGUAGE SKILLS

Vocabulary

- Paper towel
- Wax paper
- Waxy
- Tissue paper
- Wrapping paper
- Contact paper
- Sandpaper
- Flocked paper
- Newspaper
- Magazine paper
- Paper bags
- Binder
- Index cards
- Match
- Small
- Large

Questions and Things to Say

"There are many different types of paper. We see lots of different types of paper at home and at school. Here is one type of paper. It's called *wax paper*. Usually, we use wax paper at home in the kitchen. How does it feel? Does it feel sticky? We call that a waxy feeling. This is wrapping paper. It has a design on it. How does it feel different from the wax paper? Which one do you like more?"

Songs, Chants, and Fingerplays

Song: "Paper Pass"
by Kimberly Bohannon
(Tune: "I'm a Little Teapot")

It's a piece of paper.
Look and see.
What does it feel like?
What do you see?
When you pick it up
And look left and right,
Is it soft or sticky?
Is it heavy or light?

Pizza, Pizza Pie

MATERIALS

- White paper plates
- Small scraps of paper torn in 1- to 2-inch pieces
- Colored construction paper
- Glue sticks
- Crayons
- Markers

Suggested Books

- *Colors, ABC, Numbers* by Roger Priddy
- *Counting in the Garden* by Kim Parker
- *Curious George and the Pizza*
  by Margret Rey and H. A. Rey
- *How Does Your Salad Grow?*
  by Francie Alexander
- *Roar! A Noisy Counting Book*
  by Pamela Duncan Edwards

HOW TO DO IT

Let children create their own pizzas with crayons, small pieces of colored paper, and paper plates. Talk about the different vegetables and ingredients used on pizza, such as tomatoes, olives, and pepperoni. Start by having the children tear or cut small pieces of paper to make toppings. As they select toppings, talk about how they can sort and count the different pieces of paper. They can color their paper plates with crayons and markers and then glue their toppings to them. Read the suggested books, introduce the vocabulary words, and sing and chant with the children.

Modifications for Twos

Add a baker's hat, apron, rolling pin, a restaurant menu, and a clean pizza box to the dramatic play area.

LEARNING OUTCOMES

SOCIAL-EMOTIONAL DEVELOPMENT
- Sense of self
- Personal identity
- Relationships with adults
- Relationships with peers
- Self-regulation
- Sharing

PHYSICAL DEVELOPMENT
* Fine-motor skills
- Perception

COGNITIVE DEVELOPMENT
* Number awareness
- Memory
- Spatial awareness
- Connecting experiences
- Number awareness
- Imitating others
- Progression of play
- Following simple directions

LANGUAGE DEVELOPMENT
- Receptive language
- Expressive language
- Communicating needs
- Connecting words with
  real-world knowledge
- Concept words
- Using language in play

Expand the Activity

Plan a cooking activity in which children who can eat pizza make their own pizzas with English muffins, pizza sauce, and cheese. Bake the pizzas in a conventional or toaster oven. Talk about how the pizza smells when it's cooking and how the cheese melts.

BUILD LANGUAGE SKILLS

Vocabulary

- Round
- Cut
- Tear
- Glue
- Paper plate
- Pizza
- Tomatoes
- Olives
- Pepperoni
- Eat
- Bake

Questions and Things to Say

"We're going to make our own paper pizzas today. Pizzas are round. What kinds of things do we eat on pizza? Sometimes people put toppings like pepperoni, vegetables, or olives on it too. You can tear the pieces of paper to look like the toppings and glue them on the pizza. How many different colors are you using? Let's count the number of pieces of colored paper you're putting on your pizza."

Songs, Chants, and Fingerplays

Chant: "Pizza" by Kimberly Bohannon

Pizza for me.
Pizza for you.
I like pizza.
How about you?

86

Playing Together

MATERIALS

– Materials that can be used to teach sharing and empathy

Suggested Books

– *Friends at School* by Rochelle Bunnett
– *Please Play Safe! Penguin's Guide to Playground Safety* by Margery Cuyler
– *Richard Scarry's Please and Thank You Book* by Richard Scarry
– *Sharing Time* by Elizabeth Verdick
– *When I Care About Others* by Cornelia Maude Spelman

HOW TO DO IT

Children learn to share and develop empathy when adults facilitate their play activities and support their language development. Promote sharing, taking turns, and learning about empathy though everyday activities. For example, children can play together in a sandbox while you help them share shovels and sifters. Use circle time as an opportunity for children to pass objects to the sound of music. Read the suggested books, introduce the vocabulary words, and sing and chant with the children.

Modifications for Twos

Adults can facilitate the play activities of older children by building on their growing play skills. For example, in the sandbox, ask children to pass the dump truck or shovel to their neighbor. Or ask them to pick a friend to join in singing or dancing.

LEARNING OUTCOMES

SOCIAL-EMOTIONAL DEVELOPMENT
* Empathy
* Sharing
– Sense of self
– Relationships with adults
– Relationships with peers
– Self-regulation
– Caring for others

PHYSICAL DEVELOPMENT
– Gross-motor skills
– Fine-motor skills

COGNITIVE DEVELOPMENT
– Memory
– Imitating others
– Progression of play
– Following simple directions

LANGUAGE DEVELOPMENT
– Receptive language
– Expressive language
– Communicating needs
– Using language in play

Expand the Activity

Take photographs of the children playing and sharing. Post the printed photos in an area where the children can see them. Help build the children's vocabulary as you reinforce their understanding of sharing and empathy.

BUILD LANGUAGE SKILLS

Vocabulary

- Sharing
- Feelings
- Caring

- Others
- Friends
- Play

- Turns
- Pass
- Give

- Please
- Thank you

Questions and Things to Say

"Learning to share is an important part of making friends. In our classroom, we share and care for our friends' feelings. Angela and Veronica are playing together so nicely. I can see how you are sharing the blocks. Marco looks like he'd like to play with the blocks too. Marco, do you want to join us? Look how high Marco's building is."

Songs, Chants, and Fingerplays

Song: "Friends at School" by Jean Barbre
(Tune: "Frère Jacques")

Play together, play together.
Let's have fun, let's have fun.
We have fun together.
We have fun together.
Friends at school.
Friends at school.

Pop Art

MATERIALS

- Muffin tins
- Water
- Tempera paint
- Easel paper
- Large cardboard box

Suggested Books

- *The Apple Pie Tree* by Zoe Hall
- *Colors, ABC, Numbers* by Roger Priddy
- *Ice Pop Joy* by Annie Daulter
- *My Five Senses* by Aliki
- *My Five Senses* by Margaret Miller
- *Roar! A Noisy Counting Book*
  by Pamela Duncan Edwards

HOW TO DO IT

LEARNING OUTCOMES

SOCIAL-EMOTIONAL DEVELOPMENT
- Relationships with adults
- Relationships with peers
- Sharing

PHYSICAL DEVELOPMENT
- Perception
- Fine-motor skills

COGNITIVE DEVELOPMENT
* Spatial awareness
* Number awareness
- Cause and effect
- Connecting experiences

LANGUAGE DEVELOPMENT
- Receptive language
- Expressive language
- Connecting words with
  real-world knowledge
- Concept words

Note: This activity is best done outdoors on
a warm day.

Fill muffin tins with water and place them in the freezer. When the water is frozen, cover
the entire bottom of a large, sturdy cardboard box with a piece of easel paper. The paper
should cover the entire bottom of the box. The lid of a box could also be used. Squirt different colors of tempera paint on the easel paper. Then count the ice balls with the children.
Let them take turns dropping the balls, one by one, into the box. Invite the children to take
turns lifting up the ends of the box, rolling the ice balls back and forth. Describe what's
happening inside the box to the paint and the melting ice. Count the balls as they melt.
Hang up the pictures to dry. Read the suggested books, introduce the vocabulary words,
and sing and chant with the children.

Modifications for Twos

Let the children use ice balls to paint outdoors on the sidewalk. Use warm washcloths, dry
paper towels, or mittens to keep little hands from becoming cold. Once the ice is melted,

children can continue to paint with large paintbrushes. The children will get a little wet doing this activity, so it's best to do it on a sunny day.

Expand the Activity

Make ice pops. Ask the children to select an unsweetened juice. Then pour the juice into paper cups, ice cube trays, or ice-pop trays (three-quarters full). Count the individual cups or tray spaces as you fill them. Place the cups or trays in the freezer until the juice becomes slushy and holds craft sticks in place. Place the ice pops back in the freezer until completely frozen. It's best to leave them overnight in the freezer. If you are using paper cups instead, peel off the paper before serving. Show children the pictures in the book *Ice Pop Joy.* This is a great activity for a warm day in the summer.

BUILD LANGUAGE SKILLS

Vocabulary

– Balls	– Freeze	– Tray	– Sweet
– Ice	– Frozen	– Ice pops	– Cold
– Roll	– Slushy	– Stick	
– Paint	– Hard	– Drip	
– Pour	– Juice	– Thaw	

Questions and Things to Say

"Let's count the ice balls as we place them in the box. How do the ice balls feel? Are they cold? What colors of paint shall we use? Look at the paint as it gets wet. When we lift the end of the box, the ice balls roll back and forth. The paint colors are mixing together. What color does the yellow and red paint make? That's right—it's orange. What's happening to the ice balls? Let's count how many ice balls are left."

Songs, Chants, and Fingerplays

Chant: "One Pop, Two Pop" by Jean Barbre

One pop, two pop,
Three pop, four.
Five pop, six pop,
We want more.

Recycled Art

MATERIALS

- Recyclable items (such as empty cereal boxes, paper plates, plastic bottles, paper towel rolls, newspapers, and magazines)
- Glue
- Electrical tape (colored electrical tape is a little bit more expensive but adds liveliness to the sculpture)

Suggested Books

- *Big Earth, Little Me* by Thom Wiley
- *The Cleanup Surprise* by Christine Loomis
- *Not a Box* by Antoinette Portis

HOW TO DO IT

Ask families to donate recyclable items for this activity. Help children build a structure using recyclable materials. Secure the items with electrical tape and glue. Read the suggested books and introduce the vocabulary words to the children.

Modifications for Twos

Help children create their own 3-D recycled art using small scraps of construction paper, yarn, fabric, feathers, and other materials left over from other activities. Read suggested books to the children.

Expand the Activity

Read the book *Big Earth, Little Me* and discuss ways the children can learn about recycling and the importance of caring for nature and the environment.

LEARNING OUTCOMES

SOCIAL-EMOTIONAL DEVELOPMENT
- Sense of self
- Relationships with adults
- Relationships with peers
- Caring for others
- Sharing

PHYSICAL DEVELOPMENT
- Fine-motor skills

COGNITIVE DEVELOPMENT
- Spatial awareness
- Number awareness
- Progression of play
- Following simple directions

LANGUAGE DEVELOPMENT
- ✱ Expressive language
- ✱ Engaging in print
- Receptive language
- Concept words
- Using language in play

BUILD LANGUAGE SKILLS

Vocabulary

- Recycle
- Earth
- Environment
- Nature
- Boxes
- Plastic

- Paper
- Stack
- Top
- Place
- Side
- Attach

- Glue
- Stick
- Structure
- Sturdy
- Strong

Questions and Things to Say

"It's important to care about nature and our environment. We can do that by reusing things we already have. We're going to make a structure using the things you brought from home. Here's a cereal box. It has words written on it. See the letters? Let's put the boxes on the ground and build a structure together."

Sand Blast

MATERIALS

– Large plastic tub or sensory table
– Colander or sand sifter
– Plastic cups
– Sand
– Water
– Pitcher
– Hamster shavings
– Cornmeal
– Small toys (such as plastic farm or jungle animals)

Suggested Books

– *Colors, ABC, Numbers* by Roger Priddy
– *Dig Dig Digging* by Margaret Mayo
– *Richard Scarry's Best First Book Ever!* by Richard Scarry

HOW TO DO IT

Set the plastic tub on a low table and fill it with an inch of sand. Position the table so the children can view the sand as it falls through a colander or sifter. Place a variety of small toys in the plastic tub along with fine sand. Show the children how to scoop and shake the sand toys. Read the suggested books, introduce the vocabulary words, and sing and chant with the children.

Modifications for Twos

Let the children select plastic animals to be placed in the tub. Substitute the sand with a variety of different materials for the sand, such as clean hamster shavings, shredded paper, or packing peanuts.

LEARNING OUTCOMES

SOCIAL-EMOTIONAL DEVELOPMENT
– Sense of self
– Relationships with adults
– Relationships with peers
– Self-regulation
– Sharing

PHYSICAL DEVELOPMENT
✱ Perception
– Gross-motor skills
– Fine-motor skills

COGNITIVE DEVELOPMENT
✱ Spatial awareness
– Cause and effect
– Memory
– Connecting experiences
– Imitating others

LANGUAGE DEVELOPMENT
– Receptive language
– Expressive language
– Connecting words with real-world knowledge
– Concept words

Expand the Activity

Substitute the sand for water and repeat the steps. Fill a small pitcher with water and let the children pour water through the colanders. Talk about what they are seeing, and encourage them to experiment with the different materials and toys.

BUILD LANGUAGE SKILLS

Vocabulary

- Colander
- Sifter
- Scoop
- Cups
- Sand
- Water
- Fall
- Holes
- Pour
- Shake
- Through
- Over
- Hide
- Animals

Questions and Things to Say

"I'm going to scoop up the sand and place it in the colander. Watch it fall through the holes. Place your hand under the colander. See how the sand falls through your fingers? What happened to the animals? Did they fall through the holes? Can we hide them in the sand?"

Songs, Chants, and Fingerplays

Song: "Scoop, Scoop, Scoop the Sand" by Jean Barbre
(Tune: "Row, Row, Row Your Boat")

Scoop, scoop, scoop the sand.
Scoop the sand today.
Scoop it once, scoop it twice.
Scooping sand is fun!

Shoes, Shoes, and More Shoes

MATERIALS

– Children's shoes
– Two medium-size baskets

Suggested Books

– *Colors, ABC, Numbers* by Roger Priddy
– *Doggies: A Counting and Barking Book* by Sandra Boynton
– *Gray Rabbit's Odd One Out* by Alan Baker
– *Roar! A Noisy Counting Book* by Pamela Duncan Edwards

HOW TO DO IT

Explain that shoes come in pairs and that there are different kinds of shoes, such as tennis shoes or boots. Talk about the colors and types of shoes worn by the children. Identify which shoes have laces or Velcro. Ask the children to look at their own shoes and invite them to place one of their shoes in a basket. One by one, let children select their own shoe from the basket. Return all the shoes to the basket before the next child takes his turn. After all the children have taken their turns, let them find their matching shoe again. Help them put their shoes back on. Read the suggested books, introduce the vocabulary words, and sing and chant with the children.

Modifications for Twos

Help older children identify the details of the different shoes. You may want to add dress-up shoes or large boots for variety. Ask the children to sort and categorize the shoes.

LEARNING OUTCOMES

SOCIAL-EMOTIONAL DEVELOPMENT
✱ Personal identity
– Sense of self
– Relationships with adults
– Relationships with peers
– Sharing

PHYSICAL DEVELOPMENT
– Fine-motor skills

COGNITIVE DEVELOPMENT
✱ Number awareness
– Memory
– Spatial awareness
– Connecting experiences
– Imitating others
– Progression of play
– Following simple directions

LANGUAGE DEVELOPMENT
– Receptive language
– Expressive language
– Connecting words with real-world knowledge
– Concept words

Expand the Activity

Introduce new shoes to the dress-up area. Wrap new dress-up shoes in tissue paper and place them in shoe boxes. Place a couple of child-size chairs or a stool next to the shoe boxes to create a shoe store. Let the children see themselves in a mirror while they play with the new dress-up shoes.

BUILD LANGUAGE SKILLS

Vocabulary

- Shoes
- Match
- Same
- Different
- Leather
- Boots
- Tennis shoes
- Laces
- Velcro
- Tie
- Sole
- Toe
- Heel
- Feet

Questions and Things to Say

"There are different kinds of shoes. Shoes come in different colors. Some have laces and others have Velcro. We wear a shoe on each foot. Let's look at your shoes. What do we see when we look at them? How are your shoes the same? How are they different?"

Songs, Chants, and Fingerplays

Song: "Shoes, Shoes, Shoes"
by Kimberly Bohannon
(Tune: "Three Blind Mice")

Shoes, shoes, shoes!
Shoes, shoes, shoes!
Put one shoe on.
Put one shoe on.
See if you find the matching one.
Oh, shoes, shoes, shoes!
Shoes, shoes, shoes!

Shoes, shoes, shoes!
Shoes, shoes, shoes!
Put one shoe on.
Put one shoe on.
When it's your turn, you can pick one up.
Oh, shoes, shoes, shoes!
Shoes, shoes, shoes!

Chant: "One, Two, Buckle My Shoe" (traditional)

Soapy Bubbles

MATERIALS

- Plastic bucket or tub
- Dishwashing liquid
- Glycerin (found in drug stores) or corn syrup
- Eggbeater
- Measuring cups and spoons
- Bubble wands (purchased or handmade from string or chenille stems)
- Fly swatters
- Plastic berry baskets
- Plastic cookie cutters
- Vegetable strainer
- Towels

Suggested Books

- *Brown Rabbit's Shape Book* by Alan Baker
- *Bubbles, Bubbles* by Kathi Appelt
- *First 100 Words* by Roger Priddy
- *My Five Senses* by Aliki
- *My Five Senses* by Margaret Miller

HOW TO DO IT

This activity can get messy and is best done outdoors. Place 1 cup of water and 2 tablespoons of dishwashing soap in the plastic bucket. Beat the mixture with the eggbeater. Dip the wands into the soapy solution. Dip clean fly swatters, plastic berry baskets, plastic cookie cutters, and a variety of colanders into the bubble solution. Allow children to experiment with these various tools to create bubbles. Describe the bubbles to the children, and let them play. You can add 1 to 2 tablespoons of corn syrup or glycerin for a different bubble experience. For homemade bubble mixture, make it the day before and let it sit overnight. Have towels nearby to soak up spills. Read the suggested books, introduce the vocabulary words, and sing and chant with the children.

LEARNING OUTCOMES

SOCIAL-EMOTIONAL DEVELOPMENT
- ✷ Self-regulation
- Sense of self
- Relationships with adults
- Relationships with peers
- Sharing

PHYSICAL DEVELOPMENT
- Perception
- Fine-motor skills

COGNITIVE DEVELOPMENT
- Cause and effect
- Memory
- Spatial awareness
- Connecting experiences
- Imitating others
- Progression of play
- Following simple directions

LANGUAGE DEVELOPMENT
- ✷ Expressive language
- Receptive language
- Communicating needs
- Connecting words with real-world knowledge
- Concept words
- Using language in play

Modifications for Twos

Make wands from chenille stems by twisting the ends together to make a circle. Twist another around it to make the handle. For a larger wand, twist two chenille stems together, or cover the neck of a wire coat hanger with electrical tape and reshape it into a star, circle, square, or diamond.

Expand the Activity

Make colored bubbles by mixing 1 cup liquid tempera paint, 2 tablespoons of dishwashing liquid, and 1 tablespoon of liquid starch. Color and bubbles can be a bit messy, so be sure that children are wearing painting aprons. Use paint that can wash out easily. If the mixture is too thick, you can thin it with water. This is a great way to help children learn their colors.

BUILD LANGUAGE SKILLS

Vocabulary

- Bubble
- Soapy solution
- Wand
- Fly swatter
- Plastic berry baskets
- Slotted spoons
- Plastic cookie cutters
- Vegetable strainer
- Wire
- Coat hanger
- Top
- Clear
- Float

Questions and Things to Say

"We're going to make bubbles of different sizes and shapes. What do you want to use for a wand? What happens when we place the wand in the soapy water? Watch as the wind blows the bubbles. Let's see how far they will float in the sky."

Songs, Chants, and Fingerplays

Song: "There's a Bubble"
by Kimberly Bohannon
(Tune: "If You're Happy and You Know It")

There's a bubble on my hand, on my hand.
There's a bubble on my hand, on my hand.
There's a bubble on my hand.
There's a bubble on my hand.
There's a bubble on my hand, on my hand.

Additional verses:
There are bubbles in the air.
There's a bubble on my shirt.

There are bubbles everywhere.
Song: "Pop Goes the Bubble"
by Kimberly Bohannon
(Tune: "Pop! Goes the Weasel")

All around us bubbles float.
They're moving soft and graceful.
All around us bubbles float.
(Pop a bubble with your finger.)
Pop goes the bubble!

Sock Hop

MATERIALS

Suggested Books

- *Annie, Bea, and Chi Chi Dolores: A School Day Alphabet* by Donna Maurer
- *Bugs! Bugs! Bugs!* by Bob Barner
- *Colors, ABC, Numbers* by Roger Priddy
- *National Geographic Little Kids First Big Book of Animals* by Catherine D. Hughes

HOW TO DO IT

Demonstrate how you hop on both feet. Sing or chant as you hop around the room. Younger children may need an adult to hold both of their hands as they learn to hop. As children get older, they may be able to hop on one foot. Learning to hop on one foot takes practice, and children may be able to hop on one foot easier than the other. Read the suggested books, introduce the vocabulary words, and sing and chant with the children.

Modifications for Twos

Place a line of masking tape on the floor or a Hula-Hoop and let older children practice hopping on the line or hop into the hoop and back out. They can also hop to a color or shape placed on the carpet. Some carpets have shapes and colors woven into their design, and these work well for this activity.

Expand the Activity

Encourage children to practice their number awareness by counting the number of times they hop. Read the suggested books to the children.

LEARNING OUTCOMES

SOCIAL-EMOTIONAL DEVELOPMENT
- Sense of self
- Relationships with adults
- Relationships with peers
- Self-regulation

PHYSICAL DEVELOPMENT
* Gross-motor skills

COGNITIVE DEVELOPMENT
- Cause and effect
- Spatial awareness
- Connecting experiences
- Number awareness
- Imitating others
- Progression of play
- Following simple directions

LANGUAGE DEVELOPMENT
* Using language in play
- Receptive language
- Connecting words with real-world knowledge
- Concept words
- Engaging in music, rhythm, and rhyme

BUILD LANGUAGE SKILLS

Vocabulary

- Hop
- Feet
- Foot
- Right
- Left
- Together
- Toward
- Away

Questions and Things to Say

"What kinds of animals hop? Do bunnies hop? How about frogs or grasshoppers? We can hop too! Try hopping with me."

Songs, Chants, and Fingerplays

Song: "Hopping Feet" by Kimberly Bohannon
(Tune "Mary Had a Little Lamb")

Our class has hopping feet,
Hopping feet, hopping feet.
Our class has hopping feet,
All day long.
(Replace our class with the child's name.)

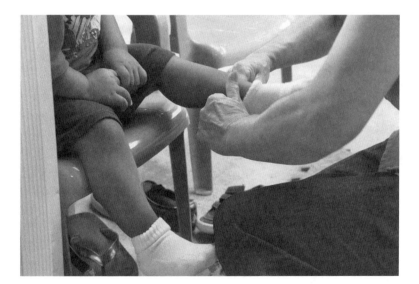

Sponge Art

MATERIALS

- Large easel
- Easel paper or white construction paper
- Paint
- A variety of new (or designated for art) kitchen sponges, loofahs, and scrub brushes

Suggested Books

- *Colors, ABC, Numbers* by Roger Priddy
- *My Hands* by Aliki
- *White Rabbit's Color Book* by Alan Baker

HOW TO DO IT

A variety of sponges add different textures and interest to the children's art. Place paint in a flat container or cups at the easel, and let the children paint with the sponges. Using one color at a time, help children learn the names of the colors. This activity can be done at an easel or on a small table as an indoor or outdoor activity. Read the suggested books and introduce the vocabulary words to the children.

Modifications for Twos

Use two primary colors at a time, and talk to the children about how two colors create new colors. For example, red and yellow make orange. Small groups of children can work side by side, sharing the paint, sponges, and brushes.

Expand the Activity

Model how to use scrub brushes with stiff bristles to splatter the paint. Add other objects, such as a fly swatter, small strainer, or slotted spatula.

LEARNING OUTCOMES

SOCIAL-EMOTIONAL DEVELOPMENT
- Sense of self
- Relationships with adults
- Relationships with peers
- Self-regulation
- Sharing

PHYSICAL DEVELOPMENT
- Perception
- Fine-motor skills

COGNITIVE DEVELOPMENT
- ★ Cause and effect
- Memory
- Spatial awareness
- Connecting experiences
- Number awareness
- Progression of play

LANGUAGE DEVELOPMENT
- ★ Engaging in print
- Receptive language
- Expressive language
- Connecting words with real-world knowledge
- Concept words
- Using language in play

BUILD LANGUAGE SKILLS

Vocabulary

– Paint	– Sponges	– Bristles
– Easel	– Loofah	– Paint
– Paper	– Scrub brushes	– Color

Questions and Things to Say

"Today, I've set up a painting area with red paint and some new things to use in painting. These are things we might see in the kitchen. Here are different kinds of sponges and scrub brushes. You can paint with them. Each one will make a different design on the paper. Which one do you like the best? Why?"

Stampin' Place

MATERIALS

- White construction paper
- Several colors of tempera paint
- Corks
- Spools of thread
- Small wood blocks
- Lids from small plastic containers (be sure they are large enough to prevent choking)
- One large new (or designated for art) sponge
- Several sponges cut into different shapes
- Clothespins
- Large unbreakable tray

Suggested Books

- *A to Z* by Sandra Boynton
- *Blue Hat, Green Hat* by Sandra Boynton
- *Colors ABC, Numbers* by Roger Priddy
- *My Hands* by Aliki
- *Richard Scarry's Best First Book Ever!* by Richard Scarry

LEARNING OUTCOMES

SOCIAL-EMOTIONAL DEVELOPMENT
- Sense of self
- Relationships with adults
- Sharing

PHYSICAL DEVELOPMENT
- ✴ Fine-motor skills
- Perception

COGNITIVE DEVELOPMENT
- Cause and effect
- Spatial awareness
- Connecting experiences
- Following simple directions

LANGUAGE DEVELOPMENT
- ✴ Engaging in print
- Receptive language
- Expressive language
- Connecting words with real-world knowledge
- Concept words

HOW TO DO IT

Place the large sponge on the tray and add paint to it. This will become the stamp pad. Show older infants and toddlers how to make stamp prints by pressing the corks, spools of thread, blocks, lids, and cut sponges onto the paint-filled sponge. Start by selecting one color at a time; then add a second color or another sponge. Place a large piece of white construction paper in front of each child and let them begin using their stamps. Read the suggested books, introduce the vocabulary words, and sing and chant with the children.

Modifications for Twos

To help children develop their fine-motor skills, attach clothespins to the sponges. Show the children how to pinch the clothespins as they stamp their picture. Add sponges cut into the shape of triangles, squares, circles, rectangles, and other shapes as well as purchased stamps.

Place a large piece of white construction paper in front of each child and let them begin using their stamps.

Expand the Activity

Dampen a piece of paper towel or coffee filter. Let the children stamp the wet paper with different paints. The colors will blend together in a rainbow.

BUILD LANGUAGE SKILLS

Vocabulary

- Sponge
- Cork
- Blocks
- Spool

- Clothespin
- Red
- Blue
- Yellow

- Green
- Orange
- Colors of paint
- Texture

- Wet

Questions and Things to Say

"What does it look like when we use the sponge? Does the design have holes and circles on it? Let's see what happens when we roll the spool of thread in the paint. What do you see on the paper?"

Songs, Chants, and Fingerplays

Chant: "Stamp, Stamp" by Kimberly Bohannon

Stamp, stamp.
Stamp this place.
See the mark on the space.
Stamp, Stamp.
One, two, three.
Stamp, stamp.
Look at me.

Stop and Go

MATERIALS

- Music
- A toy to share (such as a teddy bear)

Suggested Books

- *Friends at School* by Rochelle Bunnett
- *How Many Can Play?* by Susan Canizares and Betsy Chessen
- *Please Play Safe! Penguin's Guide to Playground Safety* by Margery Cuyler

HOW TO DO IT

Ask the children to sit in a circle. Talk about how they are going to pass the toy around the circle. Explain that the person next to them will hand them the toy, and they are to pass it to the next child. Practice this a few times without the music. Next, explain that you will start the music and when it stops, the child who is holding the toy will stop passing it. When you stop the music, say "Stop." The child will hold the toy until the music begins again. Begin the music again, say "Go," and ask the children to continue passing the toy. Repeat the process. Read the suggested books, introduce the vocabulary words, and sing and chant with the children.

Modifications for Twos

Pass two toys around the circle instead of one.

LEARNING OUTCOMES

SOCIAL-EMOTIONAL DEVELOPMENT
* Self-regulation
- Sense of self
- Relationships with adults
- Relationships with peers
- Caring for others
- Sharing

PHYSICAL DEVELOPMENT
- Gross-motor skills

COGNITIVE DEVELOPMENT
- Spatial awareness
- Connecting experiences
- Number awareness
- Imitating others
- Progression of play
- Following simple directions

LANGUAGE DEVELOPMENT
* Receptive language
- Connecting words with real-world knowledge
- Concept words
- Engaging in music, rhythm, and rhyme
- Using language in play

Expand the Activity

Help children learn to follow directions and learn about the concepts *stop* and *go*. Talk to them about what it means to stop or freeze in the middle of an activity, such as during a dancing or movement activity, and then to resume the activity when you say "Go." This also helps them learn self-regulation and anticipation of what comes next.

BUILD LANGUAGE SKILLS

Vocabulary

- Pass
- Share
- Next
- Neighbor
- Go
- Start
- Stop
- Freeze
- Hold

Questions and Things to Say

"Learning to share is important. What things do we share with our friends? We're going to share the teddy bear by passing it from one of you to the next. While we listen to the music, we'll slowly pass the bear. When the music stops, whoever has the bear gets to hold it. When the music starts again, that person will pass the bear to their neighbor."

Songs, Chants, and Fingerplays

Chant: "Stop, Look, and Listen"

Stop, look, and listen
Before you cross the street.
Use your eyes.
Use your ears.
Before you use your feet.

String It!

MATERIALS

- Heavy yarn (three-ply works best)
- Large, many-colored beads
- Tray or basket
- Scissors
- Masking tape

Suggested Books

- *Blue Hat, Green Hat* by Sandra Boynton
- *Gray Rabbit's Odd One Out* by Alan Baker
- *My Hands* by Aliki
- *White Rabbit's Color Book* by Alan Baker

HOW TO DO IT

Cut a piece of heavy yarn between 12 and 18 inches in length. Tie a knot at one end so the beads can't slide off. On the other end of the yarn, twist a piece of masking tape to make a strong, needlelike tip. Set beads in a small basket or tray on a table. Model how to string the beads, using descriptive language. This is a great activity for teaching concept words, colors, cause and effect, and beginning patterning. Young toddlers may need assistance with stringing the beads. Beads can pose a choking hazard for young children, so always supervise beading. Read the suggested books and introduce the vocabulary words to the children.

Modifications for Twos

Various sizes and colors of beads can be used for sorting. A muffin tin makes it easier to sort and keep the beads separate. Place all the beads in a basket. Help children identify the colors of beads and concept words such as *big*, *little*, *large*, and *small*. Let the children sort the beads into separate muffin cups.

LEARNING OUTCOMES

SOCIAL-EMOTIONAL DEVELOPMENT
- Sense of self
- Personal identity
- Relationships with adults
- Self-regulation
- Sharing

PHYSICAL DEVELOPMENT
* Fine-motor skills

COGNITIVE DEVELOPMENT
* Number awareness
- Memory
- Spatial awareness
- Connecting experiences
- Imitating others
- Following simple directions

LANGUAGE DEVELOPMENT
- Receptive language
- Expressive language
- Connecting words with real-world knowledge
- Concept words

Expand the Activity

Help children learn how to create a simple A-B pattern. Select two colors to bead, and model how to place beads in a pattern, such as red (A), yellow (B), red (A), yellow (B), red (A). For example, place red and yellow beads in a sequence and then ask the children which color of bead should come next. When the children have mastered this sequence, add a third bead color.

BUILD LANGUAGE SKILLS

Vocabulary

– Beads	– Point	– Twist	– Little
– Yard	– Pull	– Knot	– Large
– String	– Through	– Big	– Small

Questions and Things to Say

"We're going to put beads on a length of yarn. I'm threading the yarn through the bead and pulling it out the other side. Which bead should we use next? Oh, you picked a blue bead! See how the blue bead slips down the yarn? I'll hold the yarn while you try to string the bead."

Sunshine and Rainbows

MATERIALS

– Photographs of sunshine, rain, snow, clouds, windy days, and rainbows

Suggested Books

– *Planting a Rainbow* by Lois Ehlert
– *What Makes the Seasons?* by Megan Montague Cash
– *What Will the Weather Be Like Today?* by Paul Rogers
– *White Rabbit's Color Book* by Alan Baker

HOW TO DO IT

Talk to children about the weather and show them photographs of the sun, rain, snow, clouds, windy days, and rainbows. Describe today's weather. When you go for walks or play outdoors, mention the weather. Explain why we see rainbows, point one out, or show a picture of one. Talk about the colors of a rainbow. Read the suggested books, introduce the vocabulary words, and sing and chant with the children.

Modifications for Twos

Explain how a shadow is created when an object blocks the flow of light. Walk outdoors and point out shadows to the children. Take a prism outside or place it on a windowsill. Point out how the sunlight shines through the prism, producing the colors of the rainbow.

Expand the Activity

In a sunny place, lay a large piece of butcher paper on the sidewalk. Draw a child's shadow on the paper. Repeat this for each child. Let the children color their shadows and take them home.

LEARNING OUTCOMES

SOCIAL-EMOTIONAL DEVELOPMENT
✳ Relationships with adults
– Relationships with peers
– Caring for others
– Sharing

PHYSICAL DEVELOPMENT
– Perception

COGNITIVE DEVELOPMENT
– Cause and effect
– Memory
– Spatial awareness
– Connecting experiences
– Progression of play

LANGUAGE DEVELOPMENT
✳ Receptive language
– Expressive language
– Connecting words with real-world knowledge
– Concept words
– Engaging in print

BUILD LANGUAGE SKILLS

Vocabulary

- Sunshine
- Rain
- Snow
- Clouds
- Wind
- Rainbow
- Colors
- Prisms
- Shadows
- Light

Questions and Things to Say

"It's raining outside today. If the sun comes out while it's still raining, we might get to see a rainbow. Look—you can see it. What colors do you see?"

Songs, Chants, and Fingerplays

Song: "What's the Weather Like Today?" by Kimberly Bohannon
(Tune: "London Bridge Is Falling Down")

What's the weather like today?
Like today? Like today?
What's the weather like today?
Won't you tell me?

Chant: "Weather Watch" by Kimberly Bohannon

Sun, wind, rain, or snow.
What's the weather?
What do we know?
Sun, wind, rain, or snow.
What do you see?
What do we know?
Sun, wind, rain, or snow.
What should we wear?
What do we know?

Chant: "Rain, Rain, Go Away" (traditional)

Tom-Tom Drum

MATERIALS

– Cardboard containers, such as empty 18- or 42-ounce oatmeal boxes
– Glue
– Contact paper
– Scissors
– Crayons
– Markers
– Feathers
– Pom-poms
– Yarn
– Fabric and felt pieces

Suggested Books

– *Mouse's First Day of School* by Lauren Thompson
– *Too Loud Lily* by Sofie Laguna
– *Zin! Zin! Zin! A Violin* by Lloyd Moss

HOW TO DO IT

Collect sturdy cardboard cylinders—these will be your drums. Take off the lids, and help the children cover the containers with contact paper. Let them decorate the drums using crayons, markers, feathers, pom-poms, yarn, fabric, or felt pieces. Secure the lids on top of the drums. Encourage the children to use their hands or rhythm sticks to beat the tom-toms. Read the suggested books, introduce the vocabulary words, and sing and chant with the children.

Modifications for Twos

Each drum makes its own sound, depending on how hard or soft it's tapped and what is used to tap it. Let the children experiment with using their hands or other objects like sticks or wooden spoons to tap their drums. Talk about the different sounds and tones (for example, low or deep) each makes.

LEARNING OUTCOMES

SOCIAL-EMOTIONAL DEVELOPMENT
– Sense of self
– Personal identity
– Relationships with adults
– Relationships with peers
– Self-regulation
– Sharing

PHYSICAL DEVELOPMENT
∗ Perception
– Fine-motor skills

COGNITIVE DEVELOPMENT
∗ Following simple directions
– Cause and effect
– Memory
– Spatial awareness
– Connecting experiences
– Imitating others
– Progression of play

LANGUAGE DEVELOPMENT
– Receptive language
– Expressive language
– Connecting words with real-world knowledge
– Concept words
– Engaging in music, rhythm, and rhyme
– Using language in play

Expand the Activity

Use the tom-toms while singing a song or tapping out the syllables in the children's names, such as "Jess-i-ca."

BUILD LANGUAGE SKILLS

Vocabulary

- Tom-tom
- Drum
- Container
- Round

- Inside
- Empty
- Top
- Feathers

- Fabric
- Tap
- Beat
- Sound

- Rhythm

Questions and Things to Say

"Each tom-tom drum sounds different from the others. Let's listen to the sound each one makes. Tap the top of yours and listen to the sound it makes. How does yours sound? Is it a low sound or a high sound? Does it sound different if you place it on the ground?"

Songs, Chants, and Fingerplays

Song: "Play Make a Sound" by Jean Barbre (Tune: "This Old Man")

Make a sound,
Make a sound,
Play your instruments nice and loud.
Play them fast, play them slow,
Play them any way you know.
Now play your instruments. Here we go!

Tap your drums,
Tap your drums,
Tap your drums with a rum tum tum.
Hit them high, hit them low,
Play them any way you know.
Now play your instruments. Here we go!

Chant: "Marching Beat"
by Kimberly Bohannon

Keep the rhythm,
Yes, keep the beat.
March around
And move your feet.
Keep the rhythm,
Yes, keep the beat.
Play your drum
And move your feet.

Walk Like an Animal

MATERIALS

- Photographs and books showing farm animals and wild animals
- Music about animals (such as Greg and Steve's "Animal Action" songs from *Kids in Motion*)

Suggested Books

- *Baby Touch and Feel Animals* by DK Publishing
- *Bear Snores On* by Karma Wilson
- *Biggest, Strongest, Fastest* by Steve Jenkins
- *National Geographic Little Kids First Big Book of Animals* by Catherine D. Hughes
- *Roar! A Noisy Counting Book* by Pamela Duncan Edwards

HOW TO DO IT

Select a book about animals, such as one from the list above or one of your favorites. Read and talk about the animals in the book. Describe where the animals live, what they eat, and how they move. For example, say that most horses live on farms, make neighing sounds, eat grasses, and love apples. Demonstrate how horses walk and gallop. Ask the children to imitate the sounds horses make. Let them practice walking and galloping like horses. Introduce a second animal, such as a cow or pig, and repeat the activity. Introduce the vocabulary words, and sing and chant with the children.

Modifications for Twos

Introduce similar animals at the same time, such as five or six farm animals and then five or six jungle animals. Grouping like animals helps children see connections between animals and their habitats and environments. Help children count and sort the animals.

LEARNING OUTCOMES

SOCIAL-EMOTIONAL DEVELOPMENT
- Sense of self
- Relationships with adults
- Relationships with peers
- Caring for others
- Sharing

PHYSICAL DEVELOPMENT
- Gross-motor skills

COGNITIVE DEVELOPMENT
✶ Imitating others
- Memory
- Connecting experiences
- Number awareness
- Progression of play
- Following simple directions

LANGUAGE DEVELOPMENT
✶ Using language in play
- Receptive language
- Expressive language
- Connecting words with real-world knowledge
- Concept words
- Engaging in print
- Engaging in music, rhythm, and rhyme

Expand the Activity

Let older children make a paper-plate mask and draw their favorite animal's face with crayons or markers. Some young children do not like to put on masks and may prefer to carry theirs. Encourage children to take turns in a small group, talking about their favorite animal and showing their peers how the animal moves.

BUILD LANGUAGE SKILLS

Vocabulary

- Move
- Walk
- Crawl
- Hop
- Swing
- Jump
- Gallop
- Slither
- Swim
- Run

Questions and Things to Say

"Today we're going to look at the animals that live on the farm. First, let's look at the book with the farm animals. The horse says "Neigh." Let's say that together: "Neigh." Sometimes a horse walks, sometimes it trots, and other times it gallops. Let me show you how to gallop. Try it with me. What other animals run?"

Songs, Chants, and Fingerplays

Song: "If I Were a Farmer (Animal Sounds)"
by Kimberly Bohannon
(Tune: "The More We Get Together")

If I were a farmer, a farmer, a farmer,
Oh, if I were a farmer, I'd have a horse
Who'd say *neigh, neigh, neigh,*
Neigh, neigh, neigh.
Neigh, neigh, neigh.
Neigh, neigh.
Oh, if I were a farmer, I'd have a horse.
(Replace the horse with other animals and their sounds.)

Song: "What Sound Does a Horse Make?"
by Kimberly Bohannon
(Tune: "The More We Get Together")

What sound does a horse make?
A horse make? A horse make?
What sound does a horse make?
Please make it now.

Additional verses:
Replace horse sounds with other animal sounds.

Chant: "How Does a Horse Move?"
by Kimberly Bohannon

How does a horse move?
A horse move? A horse move?
How does a horse move?
Please show me how.

Additional verses:
Replace horse moves with other animal moves.

100

TODDLER

What Are They Rubbing?

MATERIALS

- A variety of items for making rubbings
  (such as leaves, barks, feathers, and seashells)
- Crayons
- Markers
- Tape
- Paper (lightweight paper works best)

Suggested Books

- *A to Z* by Sandra Boynton
- *Brown Rabbit's Shape Book* by Alan Baker
- *Richard Scarry's Best First Book Ever!*
  by Richard Scarry
- *White Rabbit's Color Book* by Alan Baker

HOW TO DO IT

Talk about the different items to use for rubbing,
and let the children feel them. Objects that are
relatively flat are easier for younger children. If
possible, tape the objects on a flat surface to hold
them in place. Cover the object with paper, and
demonstrate how to rub a crayon or marker over
it. The object's shape will appear. As you model the
activity, talk about the color of the crayon you're using and the shape of the object.
Read the suggested books and introduce the vocabulary words to the children.

Modifications for Twos

Help the children pick items, such as feathers, keys, coins, or seashells, to make rubbings of.
Talk about the shapes and textures of these items and how they can be seen on the paper.
Write the names of the objects, such as seashells or keys, on the children's paper.

LEARNING OUTCOMES

SOCIAL-EMOTIONAL DEVELOPMENT
- Sense of self
- Personal identity
- Relationships with adults
- Self-regulation
- Sharing

PHYSICAL DEVELOPMENT
- Fine-motor skills

COGNITIVE DEVELOPMENT
* Imitating others
- Cause and effect
- Memory
- Spatial awareness
- Connecting experiences
- Number awareness
- Progression of play
- Following simple directions

LANGUAGE DEVELOPMENT
* Engaging in print
- Receptive language
- Expressive language
- Connecting words with
  real-world knowledge
- Concept words

Expand the Activity

Select items found outdoors to use for the rubbings. Experiment with rubbing outdoors using colored chalk.

BUILD LANGUAGE SKILLS

Vocabulary

- Rubbings
- Rub
- Feather
- Key
- Coin
- Seashells
- Edges
- Bumpy
- Smooth
- Crayon
- Markers
- Chalk
- Over
- Under
- Up
- Down

Questions and Things to Say

"Look at the seashells. Each of them is special. They have bumpy edges. I'm going to place the shells under the paper. Now, I'm going to rub it with a green crayon. Can you see the shape of the shell? Let's put the paper over those keys. Now you can rub the crayon over the paper and see what happens."

101

What's the Weather Today?

MATERIALS

Suggested Books

- *Big Earth, Little Me* by Thom Wiley
- *Little Cloud* by Eric Carle
- *What Make the Seasons?* by Megan Montague Cash
- *What Will the Weather Be Like Today?* by Paul Rogers

HOW TO DO IT

Ask the children to look out the window and tell you what the weather is like today. If it's a sunny day, talk about how the sun provides us with light and warmth and helps the plants grow. If it's windy, talk about how the wind blows and listen while the wind chime rings. Each day provides opportunities to expand children's language and understanding of concept words. Help them make connections to real-world knowledge. Share the season of the year you're in with them. Read the suggested books, introduce the vocabulary words, and sing and chant with the children.

Modifications for Twos

Create a chart for every day of the month. Design an icon for the different types of weather, such as sun, wind, rain, and clouds. During circle time, ask children to place the icon that matches the weather on the chart. Read the suggested books to the children.

LEARNING OUTCOMES

SOCIAL-EMOTIONAL DEVELOPMENT
- Sense of self
- Relationships with adults
- Sharing

PHYSICAL DEVELOPMENT
- Perception

COGNITIVE DEVELOPMENT
- Cause and effect
- Memory
- Progression of play

LANGUAGE DEVELOPMENT
- ✳ Connecting words with real-world knowledge
- ✳ Concept words
- Receptive language
- Expressive language
- Engaging in print

Expand the Activity

On cloudy days, go outside and encourage the children to look at the clouds and sky. Point out how the birds fly in the sky. Let the children feel the wind and listen to the wind chimes. Have them create pictures of the sun, clouds, and sky.

BUILD LANGUAGE SKILLS

Vocabulary

- Weather
- Day
- Season
- Winter
- Spring

- Summer
- Fall
- Wind
- Sun
- Rain

- Clouds
- Rainbow
- Birds
- Fly
- Cold

- Hot
- Breeze

Questions and Things to Say

"Today is a windy day. What does it mean to be a windy day? What do we wear outside on cool, windy days? That's right, we wear our jackets. Listen to the wind chimes outside when the wind blows against them. What do they sound like to you?"

Songs, Chants, and Fingerplays

Song: "What's the Weather Like Today?" by Kimberly Bohannon
(Tune: "London Bridge Is Falling Down")

What's the weather like today?
Like today? Like today?
What's the weather like today?
Won't you tell me.

Chant: "Weather Watch" by Kimberly Bohannon

Sun, wind, rain, or snow.
What's the weather?
What do we know?
Sun, wind, rain, or snow.
What do you see?
What do we know?
Sun, wind, rain, or snow.
What should we wear?
What do we know?

Chant: "Rain, Rain, Go Away" (traditional)

Index of Activities by Learning Domain

I = Infant activity, I/T = Infant and toddler activity, T = Toddler activity

Social-Emotional Development

Physical Development

Cognitive Development

Language Development

Recommended Children's Books

Social-Emotional Development

ABC I Like Me! by Nancy Carlson

All Asleep by Joanna Walsh

Are You a Butterfly? by Judy Allen and Tudor Humphries

Baby da Vinci: My Body by Julie Aigner-Clark

Baby Face: A Mirror Book by Gwynne L. Isaacs and Evelyn Clarke Mott

Baby Faces by Margaret Miller

Baby Touch and Feel Animals by DK Publishing

Bear's Busy Family by Stella Blackstone

Bread, Bread, Bread by Ann Morris

Dino Parade by Thom Wiley

Eyes, Nose, Fingers, and Toes: A First Book All About You by Judy Hindley

Eyes and Nose, Fingers and Toes by Bendon Publishing

Friends at School by Rochelle Bunnett

From Head to Toe by Eric Carle

Hands Off! They're Mine! A Book About Sharing by Mary Packard

Hats by Debbie Bailey

Head, Shoulders, Knees, and Toes by Annie Kubler

Heartprints by P. K. Hallinan

Hello! Good-bye! by Aliki

Hello Baby: A Black and White Mirror Book by Roger Priddy

How Do Dinosaurs Play with Their Friends? by Jane Yolen and Mark Teague

How Do I Love You? by Marion Dane Bauer

How Many Can Play? by Susan Canizares

Hug by Jez Alborough

I Am Sharing by Mercer Mayer

If You Give a Mouse a Cookie by Laura Numeroff

I Love to Sleep by Amelie Graux

I'm Thankful Each Day! by P. K. Hallinan

I See Me! by Julie Aigner Clark

I See Me! by Pegi Deitz Shea

The Kissing Hand by Audrey Penn

Let's Go to Sleep! by Patricia Geis

Let's Share by P. K. Hallinan

The Little Engine That Could by Watty Piper

Lots of Feelings by Shelley Rotner

Mine! A Sesame Street Book About Sharing by Linda Hayward

Mommy Hugs by Karen Katz

Mommy's Little Star by Janet Bingham

My First Body Board Book by DK Publishing

My Hands by Aliki

My New School by Kirsten Hall

National Geographic Little Kids First Big Book of Animals by Catherine D. Hughes

On Monday When It Rained by Cherryl Kachenmeister

The Pudgy Where Is Your Nose? Book by Laura Rader

Richard Scarry's Please and Thank You Book by Richard Scarry

Sharing Time by Elizabeth Verdick

Sleep by Roger Priddy

Sleep Tight! by Sue Baker

A Splendid Friend, Indeed by Suzanne Bloom

That's What a Friend Is by P. K. Hallinan

Today I Feel Silly: And Other Moods That Make My Day by Jamie Lee Curtis

Too Loud Lily by Sofie Laguna

Too Many Toys by David Shannon

We Are All Alike—We Are All Different by Cheltenham Elementary School Kindergartners

We Are Best Friends by Aliki

What's Wrong, Little Pookie? by Sandra Boynton

When I Care About Others by Cornelia Maude Spelman

When I Miss You by Cornelia Maude Spelman

Where Is Baby's Belly Button? by Karen Katz

Who's That Baby? by Susan Amerikaner

Physical Development

Baby Touch and Feel 1, 2, 3 by DK Publishing

Baby Touch and Feel Animals by DK Publishing

Baby Touch and Feel Farm by DK Publishing

Barnyard Dance! by Sandra Boynton

Caillou Moves Around by Christine L'Heureux

Dancing Feet! by Lindsey Craig

Don't Touch, It's Hot by David Algrim

Dora's Eggs by Julie Sykes

First Steps by Lee Wardlaw

First the Egg by Laura Vaccaro Seeger

Giraffes Can't Dance by Giles Andreae

Harold and the Purple Crayon by Crockett Johnson

Here Are My Hands by Bill Martin Jr. and
John Archambault

I Am Sick by Patricia Jensen

I Can by Helen Oxenbury

Listening Time by Elizabeth Verdick

Pat the Bunny: Shake, Shake, Bunny by Golden Books

Playtime by Roger Priddy

Playtime: Push, Pull, and Play by Emma Damon

Pooh's Touch and Feel Visit by A. A. Milne

Ready, Set, Walk! by Warner Brothers

Ten Little Fingers by Annie Kubler

This Little Piggy by Annie Kubler

*Touch and Feel Adventure: Discovering Colors and
Textures* by Alexis Barad-Cutler

Touch and Feel Baby Animals by Julie Aigner-Clark

Two Eyes, a Nose, and a Mouth by Roberta
Grobel Intrater

What Can I See? by Annie Kubler

What Makes the Seasons? by Megan Montague Cash

Whose Back Is Bumpy? by Kate Davis

Wiggle and Move by Sanja Rescek

Zin! Zin! Zin! A Violin by Lloyd Moss

Cognitive Development

The Apple Pie Tree by Zoe Hall

Baby Playtime! by DK Publishing

Baby's First Sounds by Hinkler Books

Baby's First Toys by Hinkler Books

*Baby Sounds: A Baby-Sized Introduction to Sounds
We Hear Everyday* by Joy Allen

Bats on Parade by Kathi Appelt

Big Bird's Copycat Day by Sharon Lerner

Big Earth, Little Me by Thom Wiley

Boom Boom, Beep Beep, Roar! My Sounds Book
by David Diehl

Bubble Bath Baby! by Libby Ellis

The Bubble Factory by Tomie dePaola

Bubbles, Bubbles by Kathi Appelt

Bubbles, Bubbles by Sesame Street

Bubble Trouble by Margaret Mahy

Can You? Waddle Like a Penguin by Price Stern Sloan

Catch the Ball! by Eric Carle

A Children's Treasury of Songs by Linda Bleck

Cinder the Bubble-Blowing Dragon by Jessica Anderson

The Cleanup Surprise by Christine Loomis

Clifford Counts Bubbles by Norman Bridwell

Cookie See! Cookie Do! by Anna Jane Hays

Counting in the Garden by Kim Parker

Curious George and the Pizza by Margret Rey
and H. A. Rey

Curious George at the Parade by Margret Rey
and H. A. Rey

Dig Dig Digging by Margaret Mayo and Alex Ayliffe

Elmo's World: Balls! by Sesame Street

Growing Vegetable Soup by Lois Ehlert

How Does Your Salad Grow? by Francie Alexander

Ice Pop Joy by Anni Daulter

I'm Your Bus by Marilyn Singer

It's Pumpkin Time! by Zoe Hall

Let's Play Ball! by Serena Romanelli

Lots and Lots of Zebra Stripes: Patterns in Nature
by Stephen R. Swinburne

Magnificent Monarchs by Linda Glaser

Mama Zooms by Jane Cowen-Fletcher

Monkey See, Monkey Do by Helen Oxenbury

Not a Box by Antoinette Portis

Peek-a-Baby by Karen Katz

Peek-a-Boo! by Roberta Grobel Intrater

Peekaboo Baby by Sebastien Braun

Play Ball! by Apple Jordan

Play Ball! by Santiago Cohen

Playtime by Claire Belmont

Playtime Peekaboo! by DK Publishing

Please Play Safe! Penguin's Guide to Playground Safety
by Margery Cuyler

Polar Bear, Polar Bear, What Do You Hear?
by Bill Martin Jr. and Eric Carle

Pop! A Book About Bubbles by Kimberly Brubaker
Bradley

Pop-up Peekaboo! Playtime by DK Publishing

Roar! A Noisy Counting Book by Pamela Duncan
Edwards

The Sounds Around Town by Maria Carluccio

The Surprise Garden by Zoe Hall

The Three Little Pigs by Gavin Bishop

The Very Lonely Firefly by Eric Carle

What's in the Box? by Richard Powell
What Does Baby See? by Begin Smart Books
What's in Grandma's Grocery Bag? by Hui-Mei Pan
What's in the Toy Box? by Dawn Bentley
What's That Noise? by Sally Rippin
Where Is Baby's Beach Ball? by Karen Katz
Where Is My Friend? by Simms Taback
Where's Ellie? by Salina Yoon
You and Me Together: Moms, Dads, and Kids Around the World by Barbara Kerley

Language Development

101 First Words at Home by Hinkler Studios
ABCDrive! by Naomi Howland
Actual Size by Steve Jenkins
Animal Babies by Stephen Cartwright
Annie, Bea, and Chi Chi Dolores: A School Day Alphabet by Donna Maurer
Apples and Pumpkins by Anne Rockwell
Are You a Butterfly? by Judy Allen and Tudor Humphries
Are You a Ladybug? by Judy Allen and Tudor Humphries
A to Z by Sandra Boynton
Baby Animals by Garth Williams
Baby Animals in the Wild by Kingfisher
Baby Faces: Splash! by Roberta Grobel Intrater
Baby Food by Margaret Miller
Baby Happy, Baby Sad by Leslie Patricelli
Baby Mozart: Music Is Everywhere by Julie Aigner-Clark
Baby Says Peekaboo! by Dawn Sirett
Baby's World Touch and Explore: Splash-Splash by DK Publishing
Bear Feels Scared by Karma Wilson
Bear Snores On by Karma Wilson and Jane Chapman
Biggest, Strongest, Fastest by Steve Jenkins
Black and White Rabbit's ABC by Alan Baker
Blue Hat, Green Hat by Sandra Boynton
Board Buddies: Swim! by Marilyn Brigham
Brown Bear, Brown Bear, What Do You See? by Bill Martin Jr.
Brown Rabbit's Shape Book by Alan Baker
Bugs! Bugs! Bugs! by Bob Barner
Chicka Chicka Boom Boom by Bill Martin Jr. and John Archambault
A Children's Treasury of Nursery Rhymes by Linda Bleck
Clare Beaton's Bedtime Rhymes by Clare Beaton

Click, Clack, Quackity-Quack: An Alphabetical Adventure by Doreen Cronin
Colors, ABC, Numbers by Roger Priddy
Doggies: A Counting and Barking Book by Sandra Boynton
Dogs and Cats by Steve Jenkins
Dot the Fire Dog by Lisa Desimini
Eating the Alphabet: Fruits and Vegetables from A to Z by Lois Ehlert
Elmo's World: Music! by Random House
Farm Animals by Phoebe Dunn
Feelings to Share by Todd and Peggy Snow
Fingerplays and Songs for the Very Young by Random House
First 100 Words by Roger Priddy
First the Egg by Laura Vaccaro Seeger
Flaptastic First Words by DK Publishing
Goodnight Moon by Margaret Wise Brown
Gossie by Oliver Dunrea
Gray Rabbit's Odd One Out by Alan Baker
The Grouchy Ladybug by Eric Carle
Harry the Dirty Dog by Gene Zion
Hats, Hats, Hats by Ann Morris
Hippos Go Berserk by Sandra Boynton
How Do Dinosaurs Say I Love You? by Jane Yolen
Hug by Jez Alborough
If You Take A Mouse to School by Laura Numeroff
I Love You Through and Through by Bernadette Rossetti-Shustak
Little Cloud by Eric Carle
The Little Engine That Could by Watty Piper
Little Rabbits' First Farm Book by Alan Baker
Lola at the Library by Anna McQuinn
Lots and Lots of Zebra Stripes Patterns in Nature by Stephen R. Swinburne
Moo, Baa, La La La! by Sandra Boynton
Mouse's First Day of School by Lauren Thompson
Mrs. Wishy-Washy's Farm by Joy Cowley
Music: Discovering Musical Horizons by Brainy Baby Company
Music Play by H. A. Rey
My Big Animal Book by Roger Priddy
My Five Senses by Aliki
My Five Senses by Margaret Miller
My Very First Library by Eric Carle
On the Seashore by Anna Milbourne
Open the Barn Door by Christopher Santoro
Opposites by Sandra Boynton
Pat-a-Cake! Nursery Rhymes by Annie Kubler

The Pigeon Has Feelings, Too! by Mo Willems
Planting a Rainbow by Lois Ehlert
The Rainbow Fish by Marcus Pfister
Read and Rise by Sandra L. Pinkney
Richard Scarry's Best First Book Ever! by Richard Scarry
Richard Scarry's What Do People Do All Day?
    by Richard Scarry
Rosie's Walk by Pat Hutchins
A Sock Is a Pocket for Your Toes: A Pocket Book
    by Elizabeth Garton Scanlon
Some Things Go Together by Charlotte Zolotow
Splash! by Flora McDonnell
Splash! by Sarah Garland
Spot's Favorite Baby Animals by Eric Hill
Things That Move by Jo Litchfield
The Very Busy Spider: A Lift-the-Flap Book by Eric Carle

Very First Words by Felicity Brooks
The Very Hungry Caterpillar by Eric Carle
Wah! Wah! A Backpack Baby Story by Miriam Cohen
Way Down Deep in the Deep Blue Sea by Jan Peck
What Can You Do with a Paper Bag? by Judith Cressy
What Makes the Seasons? by Megan Montague Cash
What Shall We Do with the Boo-Hoo Baby?
    by Cressida Cowell
What Will the Weather Be Like Today? by Paul Rogers
Where Did the Butterfly Get Its Name? by Melvin Berger
    and Gilda Berger
Whistle for Willie by Ezra Jack Keats
White Rabbit's Color Book by Alan Baker
Whose Hat Is This? A Look at Hats Workers Wear—
    Hard, Tall, and Shiny by Sharon Katz Cooper
Whose Nose? by Jeannette Rowe

Internet Resources

Art and Creative Materials Institute (ACMI)

www.acmiart.org

Here you can find a list of nontoxic art materials certified by the Art and Creative Materials Institute. This site also lists over two hundred companies that manufacture art materials certified as nontoxic.

Center for Applied Special Technology (CAST)

www.cast.org/udl

CAST is an educational research organization offering information on the principles of universal design for learning. It includes information on how to design your early learning environment to meet the needs of all children.

Greg and Steve Jumpin' and Jammin'

www.gregandsteve.com

Musicians Greg Scelsa and Steve Millang provide a great resource for music CDs and DVDs for children from preschool age through primary school.

Hap Palmer Educational Children's Songs

www.happalmer.com

Hap Palmer is an enthusiastic musician who provides CDs to adults for teaching skills and encouraging children's imagination. Hap Palmer's enjoyable and engaging music can be found on this website.

The National Association for the Education of Young Children (NAEYC)

www.naeyc.org

NAEYC is the leading organization for those working with and advocating on behalf of children birth to age eight. This website offers information on the association and its efforts to support early childhood education professionals. This is a useful site for educational resources, current research, requirements for program accreditation, information on developmentally appropriate practices, public policy issues, and relevant publications.

The Program for Infant/Toddler Care (PITC)

www.pitc.org

This useful website offers information on PITC's philosophy, six program policies, and training opportunities.

RaffiNews

www.raffinews.com

Here you will find a great selection of CDs, books, and DVDs by Raffi Cavoukian, the singer, author, and founder of Centre for Child Honouring.

Reading Rockets

www.readingrockets.org

A great Public Broadcasting Service resource for educators looking for new strategies, lessons, activities, and ideas for helping young children learn how to read.

Toy Industry Association, Inc

www.toyassociation.org

This organization provides consumers with information about the Toy Safety Association, toys and youth entertainments, and toy safety standards.

United States Consumer Product Safety Commission (CPSC)

www.cpsc.gov

Here you will find important information on the safety of consumer products including toys, cribs, and other products used by children birth to age three.

Zero to Three National Center for Infants, Toddlers, and Families

www.zerotothree.org

This organization informs, trains, and supports professionals, policy makers, and parents working to improve the lives of infants and toddlers.